Activity Schedules for Children with Autism

Teaching Independent Behavior

All rights reserved under International and Pan American copyright conventions. Published in the United States of America by Woodbine House, Inc., 6510 Bells Mill Road, Bethesda, MD 20817. 800-843-7323. http://www.woodbinehouse.com

Cover illustration: Liz Wolfe

Library of Congress Cataloging-in-Publication Data

McClannahan, Lynn E.
    Activity schedules for children with autism : a guide for parents and professionals / Lynn E. McClannahan and Patricia J. Krantz.
    p.   cm. – (Topics in autism)
    Includes bibliographical references and index.
    ISBN-13: 978-0-933149-93-9 (pbk.)
    ISBN-10: 0-933149-93-X (pbk.)
    Autistic children—Rehabilitation. 2. Autistic children—Education. 3. Autistic children—Life skills guides. 4. Life skills—Study and teaching. I. Krantz, Patricia J. II. Title. III. Series.
RJ506.A9M426 1999
618.92'898203—dc21   98-49913
                                                                                                  CIP

Manufactured in the United States of America

10   9   8

Topics in Autism

Activity Schedules for Children with Autism

Teaching Independent Behavior

Lynn E. McClannahan, Ph.D. &
Patricia J. Krantz, Ph.D.

Sandra L. Harris, Series Editor

WOODBINE HOUSE ◆ 1999

Remembering

Peggy W. Pulleyn

1911-1996

TABLE OF CONTENTS

PREFACE

Teaching youngsters with autism to use schedules is an exciting endeavor. We take pleasure in their steps toward independence, and admire their competence.

This book celebrates the accomplishments of many young people and their families. It is dedicated to the youngest children currently receiving intervention, who are learning picture-object correspondence skills. It is dedicated to children who, after becoming proficient schedule users, entered public school classrooms and put those skills to the test, managing homework assignments and changes in school routine. It is dedicated to children and adolescents who, although still receiving specialized intervention, contribute to family life by helping with household tasks, managing their own possessions, and initiating social interaction. And it is dedicated to adults with autism (some of them now in their 30s), whose proficient use of photographic or written activity schedules supports their independence in community work places where they make valued, and valuable, contributions.

We appreciate the participation of parents and professionals who, over the course of many years, have shared their experiences and their data about teaching young people to use activity schedules at home and in relatives' homes; at preschool or school; in churches or synagogues; in dentists' and pediatricians' offices; in parks, playgrounds, and restaurants; and even during family vacations.

The intervention strategies described here are the product of a mutual endeavor with our friends and colleagues Gregory S. MacDuff and Edward C. Fenske. Our long-time cooperative relationships with them underlie the continued development of effective treatment systems that are supported by scientific data.

1 | Independence, Choice, and Social Interaction

Tim

Chin in hand, Ellen watched her three-year-old son, Tim. Surrounded by new toys, he was lying on his back on the floor, rhythmically kicking a chair leg, humming, and staring at the ceiling light fixture. They had just finished a teaching session and he had performed well, pointing to pictures of familiar objects and imitating some sounds. But as soon as the session ended, he retreated to the floor. He looked neither at Ellen nor at the toys. Tired, she debated with herself about whether to prompt him to pick up a truck and roll it across the floor. He would probably object strenuously.

Jordan

As Jordan, age 7, happily finished his after-school snack, Dana braced herself for what was about to happen. She had promised her older son, Jack, that she would watch him ride his new bike—but she knew what Jordan would do when they approached the front door. Resolutely, she took him by the hand and said, as cheerfully as possible, "Let's go outside." As she opened the door, he screamed and fell on the threshold, kicking and crying. Jack, riding down the sidewalk, said, "I knew it!" As she struggled to move Jordan away from the door, she glimpsed Jack wheeling the bike into the garage.

Kris

Larry observed his adolescent daughter from a vantage point slightly obscured by the kitchen door. Kris was still sitting on the *couch, doing absolutely nothing. He continued to watch her inactivity as he reflected. She attended a good special education program, and she had learned a lot. She knew how to make her bed, bathe, fold laundry, make her own school lunch, and play a variety of computer games, and she usually did her homework without much assistance. But she would do none of these unless he stood up, walked toward her, and gave a direction, such as, "Why don't you fix your lunch for tomorrow?"*

Introduction

Tim, Jordan, and Kris strike a familiar chord for many of us. Tim, a preschooler, displays his new skills in structured teaching sessions, but has not learned how to appropriately fill the less-structured times between teaching activities. Jordan is often pleasant and endearing when following familiar family routines, but tantrums occur when his routines are changed. And Kris, who has acquired many competencies, does nothing unless instructed by her parents or teachers. Carefully planned activity schedules can help solve these problems and many others.

Background

This book is based on more than a decade of research conducted at the Princeton Child Development Institute. In 1986, we began our studies because we observed that, although children and youths were learning many things, they frequently failed to display their skills unless someone gave a verbal instruction, modeled the desired behavior, or gestured toward materials. Sometimes, even the smallest prompts (a half-step toward a child, or an expectant look) enabled them to do the activities. But when prompts from adults were absent, they displayed stereotypy; that is, they engaged in finger play, hand flapping, vocal noise, twirling round and round, noncontextual laughter, or other repetitive behavior, or they simply waited.

We did not assume that the children were "wrong" or incapable of using the skills they had learned—instead, we assumed that it was important to examine different teaching procedures to enable them to perform activities and tasks independently.

What Is an Activity Schedule?

An activity schedule is a set of pictures or words that cues someone to engage in a sequence of activities. An activity schedule can take many forms, but initially it is usually a three-ring binder with pictures or words on each page that cue children to perform tasks, engage in activities, or enjoy rewards. Depending on the child, the activity schedule can be very detailed—breaking a task into all of its separate parts—or it can be very general, using one picture or symbol to cue a child to perform an entire task or activity. Through graduated guidance (discussed below), children are taught to open their schedule books, turn to the first page, perform the task, and then turn to the next page for cues to the next task. The goal of teaching schedule use is to enable children with autism to perform tasks and activities without direct prompting and guidance by parents or teachers.

The schedule book for Riley, age 2, contains five pages, each of which displays one picture. The pictures show a frame-tray puzzle, a color-matching game, balls that fit in a plastic tube, felt animal cut-outs and a felt board, and corn chips on a paper plate. When his mother or instructor says "It's time to do your schedule," Riley opens his picture book, points to the first picture, goes to a nearby bookcase and gets a basket that contains the puzzle shown on page one, brings the puzzle to his little table, puts the pieces in their respective places, returns the puzzle to the basket, puts the basket back on the shelf, returns to his picture book, turns the page, points to the color-matching task, and so on. The teaching proce-

(Fig. 1-1) At 31 months, Sean has nearly mastered a photographic activity schedule that contains 14 activities. Note that his schedule book is nearby, and is open to the page that displays the picture of pegs and pegboard.

(Fig. 1-2) Because he cannot yet put the shape box away without help, Sean's father steps forward to use a prompting procedure called graduated guidance. (This procedure is discussed in Chapter 4.)

dures enable Riley to do five activities without help from his parents or instructors. Although still a toddler, he engages in independent play for ten to fifteen minutes. Before he learned to use his picture schedule, he did not play—instead, he briefly picked up toys and mouthed them, then dropped them and went on to do the same with other play materials.

Page, age 12, read at the second-grade level, and quickly acquired new sight words. After school, she followed a written schedule—a list of activities to be accomplished. Some of the activities on her list were: vacuum my room, reading homework, make pudding, fold towels, math homework, piano, exercise video, set table. Page pointed to the first item on the list ("vacuum my room"), obtained the necessary materials, and began. After completing each activity, she returned to her schedule and placed a check mark beside that item. Before new activities were added to Page's schedule, her teachers presented the new words on flash cards, and helped her learn to read them.

Many of the activities in Page's schedule were originally taught as separate lists; for example, in an earlier version of her activity schedule, the task of making pudding was separated into 19 written instructions, such as "get milk," "get bowl," and "get pudding mix." Following a written activity schedule enabled Page to use after-school time to practice new skills and to help with household tasks. Before she became a proficient schedule follower, she often spent after-school hours making perseverative demands on family members, and screaming if she did not get her way.

Independence

Riley and Page are examples of the independence that children gain when they learn to follow activity schedules. Riley's mother no longer has to monitor him continuously and remove toys from his mouth, and Page's parents don't have to give constant verbal instruction or respond to her repetitive demands. The activity schedules decreased the need for adult prompting and guidance. These results were achieved with special teaching procedures.

One of our first investigations of activity schedules (MacDuff, Krantz, & McClannahan, 1993) was conducted in one of the Princeton Child Development Institute's family-style group homes. The four boys (ages 9 to 14) who participated in the study had learned many home-living skills, such as vacuuming, dusting, table setting, doing puzzles, playing with toys, and riding bikes. But they did not do these activities unless verbally instructed, and when staff members' prompts were withdrawn, they were often "off-task"—not engaged in any appropriate activity.

Using a teaching procedure called graduated guidance, we taught the boys to follow photographic activity schedules that depicted six different leisure and homework activities, such as

Lego blocks, Perfection game, handwriting worksheets, and Tinker Toys. For example, when a youth turned to a page of his schedule book that displayed a picture of a Tinker Toy car, he learned to point to the picture, take the Tinker Toys off the shelf above his desk, assemble the car as shown in the picture, put the Tinker Toys back in the box, return the box to the shelf, and turn to the next picture in his schedule. Because these boys already knew all the steps necessary to complete each activity, their activity schedules did not cue them to do each separate step, although for other children we often create activity schedules that do that.

When the boys were doing the activities depicted in their schedule books without much help, we carefully faded the instructor's guidance, and finally, his presence. Near the end of the study, although we changed the order of the photographs and even added new photographs, the boys continued to follow their schedules without prompts from adults and, on average, they were "on-task" or appropriately engaged during 91% to 99% of our observations.

These youths, who previously experienced considerable difficulty in pursuing and finishing activities, and in making transitions from one activity to the next, now independently completed six different activities without adult help! They looked very competent.

Choice

Imagine yourself transported to another culture. You do not understand the language spoken there, and do not have a guide or translator. People ask you where you would like to go and what you would like to do, but you cannot comprehend or respond to these questions. This scenario describes the plight of many youngsters with autism who, because of their severe language deficits, are unable to participate in decisions about their own activities and daily schedules. Not surprisingly, this lack of control over the events of daily life often appears to be associated with tantrums and disruptive behavior—we would probably tantrum too if we were never allowed to decide when to eat, what task to do next, or which leisure activity to select.

Photographic and written activity schedules provide a framework for helping children with autism learn to make choices. If

(Fig. 1-3) Brent, age 9, begins each school day by sequencing his own activities and writing them in his daily planner. After completing an activity in his written schedule, he checks it off and goes on to the next task. If an activity requires the teacher's assistance, he requests help. The word "talk" cues him to initiate conversation with others in his classroom. (Procedures for teaching social interaction skills are described in detail in Chapter 10.)

we provide careful and systematic instruction, they not only learn to follow schedules, but they also learn to sequence their own activities, and to choose leisure activities that follow structured teaching sessions, homework, or home-living tasks.

Social Interaction

Pursuing our daily activities inevitably requires social exchange. But social interaction is a key deficit for children with autism, and one that should be addressed as soon as possible. Although discrete-trial training is often used to teach children with autism to imitate words, phrases, and sentences and to make verbal responses when requested to do so, this approach is not representative of the give-and-take of ordinary conversation. In discrete-trial teaching, the parent or teacher asks a question or gives an instruction and waits for the child to respond. And youngsters learn to respond and then wait for the next instruction. Indeed, many children appear to become dependent upon adults' verbal prompts—instead of initiating social interaction, they wait for others to do so. But in typical conversation, either partner may initiate, often with observations or comments, rather than with questions or directions, and one person may make several statements before the other replies.

Teaching children to use activity schedules creates a different framework for building social interaction skills, and sets many occasions for children to initiate conversation, rather than merely responding to others' instructions or queries. We recommend that even the first schedule for the youngest preschooler include at least one simple interaction task. A child who has not yet acquired language may learn to point to a picture in a schedule book and approach a parent for a toss in the air; a youngster who now has a few words may seek out a family member to say "Hi" or request "Tickle"; and a boy or girl who uses sentences may initiate conversation by requesting a preferred activity ("I want hug"), or reporting on a recently completed activity ("I did puzzle").

Our experience in early intervention programs, preschool, school, and group homes indicates that social interaction activities should be included in every activity schedule, and should be extended and elaborated as soon as possible. This theme will reappear in several subsequent chapters, together with specific suggestions about how to use activity schedules to build conversation skills.

We All Use Schedules

We are busy people. We have many commitments and we use schedules to help us accomplish our various responsibilities. We use appointment books, day timers, planners, or calendars. We use "to-do" lists that we post on the refrigerator or keep in a pocket, wallet, or purse. Some of us use electronic appointment books or computer software to keep track of our obligations.

Photographic and written activity schedules serve precisely the same function for children, youths, and adults with autism. Schedules remind them of the tasks that must be accomplished so that they, like us, need not depend upon other persons to instruct or "nag" about things that need to be done.

We would be very reluctant to give up our appointment books. Similarly, we do not ask young people with autism to give up their schedules. Instead, we help them acquire skills that enable them to use schedules that are increasingly like our own. Later we will discuss teaching procedures that help children make the transition from photographic to written schedules, and from written schedules to day timers or appointment books.

About this Book

This book is designed to introduce you to activity schedules and guide you as a parent or professional as you teach your child with autism to follow an activity schedule. Although many of the examples pertain to children, we have also included some examples relevant to adolescents and adults. It is never too late to help your son or daughter or student become more independent.

Chapter 2 discusses the skills that young people need before they begin first activity schedules, and explains how to teach these important prerequisites. Chapter 3 describes how to construct an activity schedule that is especially suited to your child's strengths. Chapter 4 provides detailed information about the teaching procedures, and Chapter 5 shows you how to measure your child's schedule-following skills. Chapter 6 explains what to do after your child masters the first schedule (with special emphasis on changing the sequence of photographs, adding new photographs, and gradually decreasing supervision). Chapter 7 addresses activities that have no clear ending (watching TV, for example), and describes how to help your child learn when to end one activity and move on to the next. Chapter 8 explains how to teach children to select their own rewards and sequence their own activities, and Chapter 9 takes a look at how children learn to follow written, rather than pictorial schedules. Chapter 10 focuses on using activity schedules to expand social interaction skills and Chapter 11 helps you troubleshoot problems with schedule following.

Time and effort are required to construct children's schedules, to teach them to follow schedules, and to systematically decrease supervision, so that they can learn to be more independent and productive, and spend less time engaging in dysfunctional behavior (Krantz, MacDuff, & McClannahan, 1993). But many parents and teachers find that the investment in teaching photographic or written activity schedules is well worth the effort.

Gordie

After returning the coloring book and crayons to a bookcase, Gordie turned a page of his schedule book and studied the next photograph, a picture of him and his sister eating cookies. His sister Gwen, age 8, glanced in his direction and interrupted the game she was playing with a friend to confide, "My brother used to ignore me, but now he talks to me, sometimes." Entering the kitchen, Gordie said, "Mom, cookies please." Seconds later, with cookies in hand, he approached his sister and said, "Cookie."

Elliott

Elliott waved goodbye to his job coach, entered his apartment, went directly to his desk, and opened his appointment book to a paper-clipped page. The first item on his written schedule that he had not yet checked off was "take out trash." Returning from the dumpster a few minutes later, he put a check mark by that item and read the next, "iron work shirts and pants." Before going to get the ironing board, he glanced down the list and read, "call grandpa" and "plan menus."

<table>
<tr><td>

2

</td><td>

Prerequisite Skills: Is My Child Ready for an Activity Schedule?

</td></tr>
</table>

Introduction

Children must learn certain skills, such as distinguishing a picture of an object from a background and matching identical objects, before they can learn to use activity schedules. Other skills not critical to learning to use activity schedules, such as putting materials away, can be acquired at the same time a child is learning to follow a schedule. This chapter discusses the skills that are necessary and makes suggestions about how to teach them; it also describes other skills that are likely to facilitate teaching and learning.

Identifying Picture versus Background

Some youngsters with autism may not yet have learned that, when presented with a picture or photograph mounted on a plain background, they should attend to the picture and not the background. Of course, in order to follow photographic activity schedules, children must learn that it is the pictures, not the backgrounds, that require scrutiny. You can assess your child's skills in this area by making a simple book, using construction paper and self-adhesive stickers that depict familiar objects. Put ten pieces of construction paper (all the same color) in a three-ring binder. Then apply one sticker per page—but put each sticker in a different location. For example, the sticker on page one may be in the upper-left corner, the sticker on page two may be in the middle of the page, and so on. Slide each page into a plastic page protector. These are useful because they extend the life of the book, and they also discourage children from attempting to remove the stickers.

Sit beside your child at a table or desk, open the book to page one, and ask, "Where's the picture?" or say, "Point to the picture." Wait five seconds, and then mark "plus" (+) on a data sheet (see Figure 2-1 and Appendix A) if your child touched the sticker during that time, or "minus" (-) if he did not touch the sticker. Score the first response your child makes on each page; for example, if he touches the background first, and then touches the sticker, score minus. If your youngster touches the stickers on

Fig. 2-1 | Identifying Picture versus Background
Data Sheet for Duane

Opportunity#	Task	Date/Time	Date/Time	Date/Time
	Picture Versus Background	1/18/98 11a.m.	1/18/98 4 p.m.	1/19/98 4:30 p.m.
1		-	-	+
2		-	-	-
3		+	-	+
4		+	+	+
5		-	-	+
6		-	+	-
7		-	+	+
8		-	+	+
9		+	+	+
10		+	+	+
Number Correct		4	6	8

(Fig. 2-1) Sample data sheet used to measure a child's skills in identifying picture versus background. Blank data sheets are included in Appendix A.

at least eight of the ten pages, you can probably assume that picture-versus-background skills have already been acquired.

If your son or daughter cannot yet do this task, you can teach it. Reserve a special snack or toy for those times when you will look at the sticker book together, and plan to do this activity several times each day. After you say, "Point to the picture," try to anticipate your child's response, so that you can prevent errors by gently but quickly guiding his hand to the sticker. If you have to help, give lots of enthusiastic praise ("Good, you found the picture"), but don't provide the preferred toy or snack—reserve these for the occasions when he makes a correct response all by himself.

Throughout this book, there are many references to edible rewards, such as raisins, popcorn, and cereal. Early in intervention, many youngsters with autism do not value praise, attention, or toys, and preferred snacks may therefore be important rewards. However, if your child enjoys stickers, stars, coins, or activities such as patty cake, peek-a-boo, or tickles, it is certainly appropriate to use these as rewards.

Matching Identical Objects

Children who are fluent and successful schedule-followers have learned that a picture of an object corresponds to an object. For example, a picture of a Big Bird toy represents the stuffed toy. But before they learn picture-object correspondence skills, children learn matching skills; that is, they learn to identify objects that are identical. It is often easier for youngsters with autism to learn to match identical three-dimensional objects, such as two bananas or two cups, before they learn to match two-dimensional objects, such as two identical stickers, or two cut-out red circles.

To determine whether your child can match identical objects, sit with her at a table or desk, and arrange five different toys or household objects on the work surface. Put five identical objects out of her sight (in your lap or pocket, or on the floor beside you). Display one of your objects (for example, a spoon) on the tabletop and say, "Point." After she points to the object you placed directly in front of her say, "Find." If your youngster reaches for, touches, or picks up the matching object within five seconds of your instruction, score this as a correct response (see Figure 2-2 and Appendix A). If she does not respond, responds after five seconds, or touches the wrong object before touching or picking up the correct object, score an incorrect response. Continue until you have provided ten opportunities for matching. Children who have learned matching skills can usually make correct responses on eight of ten opportunities; some errors may occur because of inattention. If your child hasn't yet learned to match identical objects, you can teach her by using the manual guidance, praise, and special rewards procedures described above.

Fig. 2-2 | Matching Identical Objects
Data Sheet for Judy

Opportunity#	Task	Date/Time	Date/Time	Date/Time
	Matching Identical Objects	1/27/98 3:45 p.m.	1/28/98 4 p.m.	1/29/98 4:30 p.m.
1	Sock	-	-	-
2	Spoon	-	+	+
3	Ball	+	+	+
4	Pencil	+	+	+
5	Bar of soap	-	-	-
6	Ball	+	+	+
7	Sock	-	+	+
8	Pencil	+	+	+
9	Bar of soap	-	-	-
10	Spoon	+	-	+
Number Correct		5	6	7

(Fig. 2-2) Sample data sheet used to measure a child's skills in matching identical objects. Blank data sheets are included in Appendix A.

Picture-Object Correspondence Skills

A child who has picture-object correspondence skills has learned that pictures represent depicted objects. These skills are central to the use of photographic activity schedules, but many children with autism require special instruction to help them learn the relationships between objects and pictures.

In order to measure your child's skills, make another "book" by placing five pieces of construction paper (all the same color) in a three-ring binder. Then photograph five familiar objects or cut out five magazine pictures, mount one on each page of the book, and collect five objects that are identical to those in the pictures. For example, you may find a picture of your child's favorite beverage, and purchase a bottle of that beverage. A toy

(Fig. 2-3) To teach picture-object correspondence, model pointing to the picture, say "Point," and guide the child's hand to point to the picture. Then say "Find," and guide the child to pick up the corresponding object and place it on the page.

catalog may contain a picture of a doll or car that is among your child's toys. Or an advertising circular may show a picture of a towel that is identical to your towels. The objects you collect should be exactly the same as those in the pictures, and each picture should show only the target object, and no other objects.

Sit beside your child and put the book and the objects on a work surface in front of him. Open the book, and model by pointing to the first picture, while you say, "Point." If necessary, guide your child's hand to help him point to the picture. Then say, "Find," and guide your child to pick up the target object. Immediately after he picks up an object that corresponds to the picture, praise him and give him special attention—for example, clap for him, whistle, toss him in the air, or give him a hug, kiss, or tickle. Repeat this procedure on each page of the book.

The next time you use the book, give the instructions "Point" and "Find," and wait five seconds for your child to respond. Score his response as correct if he finds the target object within five seconds and without your help; score it as incorrect if he does not respond within five seconds, does not pick up the target object,

Fig. 2-4 | Picture-Object Correspondence
Data Sheet for Roger

Opportunity#	Task	Date/Time	Date/Time	Date/Time
	Picture-Object Correspondence	2/9/98 5 p.m.	2/9/98 7 p.m.	2/10/98 4:30 p.m.
1	Truck	-	-	-
2	Cup	-	+	+
3	Shoe	-	-	-
4	Block	-	-	+
5	Toothbrush	+	+	+
Number Correct		1	2	3

(Fig. 2-4) Sample data sheet used to measure a child's picture-object correspondence skills. Blank data sheets are included in Appendix A.

or picks up an object that does not correspond to the picture (see Figure 2-4 and Appendix A).

If your youngster does not make correct responses on at least three of the five tasks, you will probably want to use the book to teach picture-object correspondence. Return to the procedures you used when you first introduced the book. Model pointing to the picture and guide your child to point to it and then pick up the corresponding object; follow this with enthusiastic praise and attention. Over a period of time, gradually withdraw your guidance. When he finds an object without your help, give him a special snack or toy, as well as praise and affection.

When your child makes correct responses on each page, it is time for a new book. Select different pictures and objects, and measure your son's responses the first time you present the new book. If he does not respond correctly on three of the five pages, continue to teach until he can do all of the tasks in the second book without your help. Continue to make new books and assess his progress until he achieves at least three of five correct responses the first time you present a new book.

Accepting Manual Guidance

The procedures we use to teach children to follow activity schedules emphasize manual guidance. If we are to accomplish this teaching, children must permit us to touch their hands, arms, and shoulders, and must allow us to guide them. Many youngsters do not display any signs of discomfort when they are physically guided by a parent or teacher, but a few respond by screaming, crying, resisting, or attempting to flee.

Observe your child when you are assisting her with tasks she has not yet mastered, such as putting her shoes on, pulling up her underwear, brushing her teeth, or using a spoon. Does she object if you put your hands over hers and help her with these activities? Children who appear comfortable with this type of assistance usually respond well to the type of instruction used in teaching activity schedules.

If your child resists manual guidance, there are several things you can do to teach her to be more receptive to your help. What kind of physical contact does she enjoy? If she likes tickles, piggy-back rides, tosses in the air, or being rocked in your lap, try to introduce a small amount of manual guidance each time you share these activities, and gradually increase your guidance over a period of days. For example, take her hand and show her how to tickle you before you tickle her. Or manually guide her to climb on a bed or chair before you begin the piggy-back ride.

You may also want to pair your manual guidance with pre-ferred toys or snacks. Guide her hand to pick up a special snack food, and gradually increase your physical contact over time. Put a special toy on a high shelf and, as you lift her up, guide her hand to reach for it. On each of these occasions, try to use the maximum amount of manual guidance that your child can tolerate without exhibiting unwanted behavior such as resisting, cry-ing, or hitting. These tactics ultimately enable most children to accept manual prompts.

Using Materials

It is helpful if a preschooler can string beads, or can com-plete puzzles, but these skills are not essential to the introduction of first photographic activity schedules. In fact, youngsters often acquire new work or play skills at the same time that they learn to follow activity schedules. But your child may learn more quickly if you can identify some activities that he has already mastered. Can he put shapes in a shape box? Can he sort picture cards into categories? Can he put the knives, forks, and spoons in their re-spective places in the kitchen drawer? If he can do these or simi-lar tasks, you may want to include them in his first schedule. Steven, age 3, had learned to drop blocks in a toy mailbox, to sort plastic horses and sheep into separate containers, and to assemble nesting cups. By including these familiar tasks in his first photographic activity schedule, his teacher made it easier for him to develop schedule-following skills.

Summary

In this chapter, we made some suggestions about how to measure and if necessary teach prerequisite skills that help a child begin a first photographic activity schedule. But there are many ways to begin. We know some young people who simultaneously learned picture-object correspondence skills and schedule-following skills. Although it took them longer to master their first schedules, they are competent schedule users today. However, time spent teaching children to identify picture versus background, to match identical objects, and to identify objects that correspond to pictures is typically time well-invested, because these skills facilitate schedule following.

3 | Preparing a First Activity Schedule

Brook

Before her teacher constructed her first schedule, Brook, age 6, had already learned to put pegs in the Lite Brite, to color simple shapes, and to give someone a "high five," but she only engaged in these activities when instructed by someone to do so. Her first schedule book included five photographs. The first three pictures showed: 1) the Lite Brite and pegs, 2) crayons and a page to be colored, and 3) Brook giving a teacher a "high five." Two other photographs showed unfamiliar activities: 4) bristle blocks and 5) raisins on a paper plate. The photographs were mounted in her schedule book, one picture to a page, and the actual materials depicted in the photos were arranged on a bookshelf near her desk. After a few weeks of teaching, Brook dependably responded to her teacher's instruction to "Find something to do"; she opened her schedule book, pointed to the first picture, got the Lite Brite and pegs from a container on the bookshelf, assembled the pegs to create a picture, put the materials away, returned to her schedule, turned the page, pointed to the picture of crayons, and so on. After pointing to the picture of "high five," she approached her teacher with hand raised, and her teacher used this interaction to provide praise and attention. When she arrived at the last photograph in the book, Brook brought the paper plate to her desk, ate the raisins, and threw the paper plate in the wastebasket. Previously she was unable to do any activities without teachers' assistance; using her first photographic activity schedule, she remained appropriately engaged with play and learning activities for about twenty minutes.

Selecting Activities

Children learn schedule-following skills more rapidly if some of the activities in the first schedule are familiar or already mastered. It is also helpful to keep the initial schedule brief; plan to begin with no more than five or six activities.

A first photographic schedule for a preschooler might include a frame-tray puzzle, stacking cups, requesting a toss in the air, shapes and shape box, and a preferred snack. A schedule for

a six- or seven-year-old might include work and play activities such as tracing lines on a worksheet; arranging letters or numerals in sequence on a magnetic board; requesting a tickle; assembling a toy, such as a Lego car or a Mr. Potato Head; and having a preferred snack. And a first schedule for a

(Fig. 3-1) Riley, age 2, puts shapes in a box without help.

ten-year-old might include some typical after-school activities, such as hanging up his jacket; using the toilet; washing his hands; putting away items in his lunch box (for example, putting the thermos on the kitchen counter, food containers in the dishwasher, and cold pack in the freezer); reporting that he has put things away; and getting his own after-school snack. It is important to select activities that are age-appropriate, so that when your son or student is independently following his schedule, he will appear skillful and competent.

You should also select activities that have clear endings, so that your youngster will know when each task is completed. A frame-tray puzzle is completed when all of the pieces are in place; a peg-board activity is finished when all the pegs are in the board (you can

can adjust the difficulty of this task by supplying a larger or smaller number of pegs). A worksheet is finished when all the tracing tasks are done, or when all of the shapes are colored, and you can adjust task length and complexity when you construct the worksheet.

In selecting activities, you may rely on local toy stores or school supply catalogs, or you may create curriculum materials that are relevant to your family, or that reflect your child's current skills and interests. For example, using tag board or file folders and Velcro, you can design matching tasks (mounting the letters "M," "o," and "m," over identical letters that are displayed under a photograph of mother). Or, you can design numeral-object correspondence tasks (mounting the numeral "2" by a picture of two dogs, and the numeral "5" by a picture of five dinosaurs).

(Fig. 3-2) A numeral-object correspondence task.

The first schedule should end with a snack or play activity that is especially enjoyable for your child. It is best to reserve this special treat for those times when your child is using his schedule; do not make this preferred food or activity available at other times.

After you have identified the activities that will be included in the first schedule, consider how to make it easy for your youngster to pick them up and put them away. Plastic dish pans, plastic baskets, or shoe boxes are often helpful in packaging materials so that young children are less likely to drop them. These containers minimize the loss of small pieces, and assist children in learning to return materials to designated locations.

Taking Pictures

You don't have to be a photographer to take the pictures that will be displayed in the schedule, but a few simple rules are important. Photographs should show only the target materials or activity, and should not include objects or events that might be confusing or distracting. Materials should be photographed against a plain background, and target objects should almost fill the frame. And pictures that are over- or under-exposed or out of focus should be discarded.

If you aren't an experienced photographer, you may find it helpful to take pictures outdoors on a bright day. Use a solid-colored carpet remnant, a piece of plywood, a large piece of tag board or foam board, a solid-colored table top, a sidewalk, or some other non-reflective surface to create a plain background. Light shade is helpful in getting a good exposure without getting your shadow in the picture.

Arrange all of the materials associated with one activity on the plain background and, when possible, arrange them to show how they are used. For example, you might photograph a five-piece puzzle with four pieces in place, and the fifth beside the puzzle. If stacking cups will be kept in a plastic basket, you may decide to photograph the cups in or beside the basket, or you may show some of the cups in the basket and others beside it. If a preschooler's snack is a few M&M's on a paper plate, photograph the candy on the plate, just as it will be presented. If a ten-year-old will get her own snack, photograph the full juice glass, the cookies, and the cookie plate that you want her to obtain.

Professional photographers "bracket" their exposures—that is, they take one picture at what appears to be the best camera setting, and then take two more at faster or slower shutter speeds, or larger or smaller lens aperture settings. You may also want to experiment with several shots of the same materials, and later select the best picture.

Because film processing can be expensive, many parents and professionals maintain libraries of negatives and unused photographs. Although a child masters her first schedule and goes on to new activities and materials, components of previous schedules may later be used to construct special schedules that can be used during vacation travel, visits to the pediatrician's office, or trips to relatives' homes. A photograph of a Lego car to be assembled may be removed from a youngster's schedule book and replaced with a photograph of a more complex model-building task, but the old picture and materials may become part of a schedule that is used at Grandma's house.

Preparing Materials

After you have collected the materials for the activity schedule, assemble them. Depending upon your child's size, age, and motor skills, you may decide to display the photographs in a 9-by-12 or a 7-by-9-inch binder, or even in a small photo album. Three-ring binders are useful because they lay flat when open, so that a child does not "loose his place."

Insert pieces of construction paper into five or six plastic page protectors, and put the page protectors in the binder. All pages should be identical, so that the color of the page, or other

(Fig. 3-3) A first photographic activity schedule. The pictures are encased in plastic baseball-card holders, and the holders are attached to schedule pages with Velcro.

irrelevant stimuli, will not interfere with your child's attention to the pictures. Place each picture in a plastic sleeve; clear plastic baseball card holders, available from hobby shops, are convenient for this purpose.

Finally, attach a Velcro circle or square to the center of each binder page, attach the matching Velcro to the back of each plastic photo holder, and mount the pictures in the schedule book. This will make it possible to change the order of the photographs after your child has mastered a first schedule. We discuss the importance of resequencing photographs in a later chapter.

Select an activity sequence that offers variety. Children's interest may flag if they are asked to do three puzzles, or complete four pages of connecting the dots. If a child will do two worksheet tasks, separate them with a different activity, such as folding towels or building a model. And remember, the preferred snack or activity should be the last picture in the schedule.

Fig. 3-4 | Preparing a First Activity Schedule
Materials Needed

SCHEDULE	TOKEN SYSTEM
Camera	Clipboard
Film	Pennies
Non-reflective background	Velcro circles
Materials included in the schedule	
Three-ring binder or album	**SOCIAL INTERACTION ACTIVITIES**
Plastic page protectors	Language Master *
Construction paper	Language Master cards *
Velcro circles or squares	
Photographs	**HOME ENVIRONMENT**
Baseball card holders	Bookcases, shelves, or desk surface
	Bins, baskets, or dishpans

* *Language Master and Language Master cards are optional; it is possible to substitute photographs or text.*

Identifying and Preparing Rewards

What rewards does your youngster presently enjoy? Does she receive bites of favorite foods as rewards for good performance? Is she accustomed to stars, stickers, happy faces, or other types of token rewards? You can begin a first activity schedule even if your child has not yet learned to value tokens, but her progress will be more rapid if you teach her to use a token system.

There are many advantages associated with the use of coins as tokens. This reinforcement procedure teaches children to value money, and can also be used to teach them to identify and count coins, and to use an allowance system like the one you may use with your other children. (Of course, if your youngster puts small objects in her mouth, you should select larger tokens, such as poker chips, blocks, or puzzle pieces).

Teaching a child to use a token system can often be accomplished in only a few sessions. Select a familiar teaching activity, and use rewards that you typically deliver. Perhaps you are teach-

(Fig. 3-5) A token system that uses pennies. Pennies are attached to the clipboard with Velcro.

ing your child to point to or label pictures of family members, pictures of common objects, or alphabet letters, and you reward correct responses with musical toys and bites of cookie or pretzel. Conduct your teaching session as usual, but when your child makes a correct response, give her a coin and quickly say, "Give me penny, and I'll give you cookie," while manually guiding this exchange. As soon as possible, ask for two responses and give your daughter two pennies before making the exchange. Then gradually increase the number of pennies needed to obtain the cookie, pretzel, or toy.

Your child will learn to value coins as a result of the consistent pairing of a preferred item (bites of cookie) and a new item (pennies). By gradually increasing the number of pennies needed for an exchange, you will help to counteract performance problems that occur when a child tires of the available rewards. There are limits on the number of cookies or pretzels any of us wants to consume on a given occasion.

To construct a monetary token system, purchase a small (6-inch by 9-inch) clipboard and find the pennies that accumulate in your purse or dresser drawer. Attach circular adhesive Velcro hooks to the back of each penny, and place the adhesive Velcro loops on the clipboard. Use the number of pennies that your child typically earns before exchanging tokens for a preferred food, toy, or activity. Placing a strip of Velcro on the edge of the clipboard provides a convenient way to store the pennies when they are not in use.

Designing the Environment

A goal for many parents is teaching children to pick up after themselves, and to put things away. This is a reasonable expectation for your son with autism, as well as for his siblings. But children cannot put things away if they do not know where toys, clothing, food, and learning materials belong. Teaching your child to follow a first activity schedule presents an opportunity to teach him that the materials he uses should be returned to designated places. Helping him acquire this important skill requires organizing his living and learning environment.

Before you begin to teach schedule following, identify an appropriate setting (his classroom, his bedroom, the living room, or the family room) and make materials easily accessible by placing them (in sequence, from left to right) on a shelf, bookcase, table, or desk. Materials should be within the child's reach, and there should be ample space to return a basket or box to the shelf after completing an activity. If space is not currently available, you may want to purchase a bookcase or some shelving. If you plan to teach an after-school schedule (described above), identify kitchen cupboards, drawers, and refrigerator shelves where plates, cookies, napkins, and juice will always reside.

Preparing to Teach Social Interaction Skills

Gordon, a preschooler with autism, offers some examples of how to include social interaction in activity schedules. At two years of age, he learned to follow his first photographic activity schedule. A picture of blowing bubbles was mounted in his schedule book, and because he had not yet learned to talk, he was taught to remove the photograph from his book and present it to his mother or father, who responded with simple language models ("Bubbles!" or "Bubbles are fun!") and then blew bubbles that Gordon enjoyed catching. By the time he was three, Gordon had

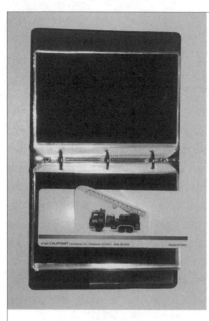 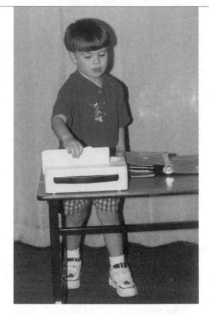

(Fig. 3-6) Gordon's schedule contains a picture of a firetruck, attached to a language master card.

He runs the card through the machine and hears the script, "Watch me."

learned to imitate words and phrases, and his parents began to use a Language Master. Special cards with strips of audiotape at the bottom were pre-recorded by his parents, pictures of social activities were attached to the cards, and the cards were attached to pages of his schedule book. One card displayed a photograph of a favorite toy, a fire truck. Gordon learned to remove the card from his book and run it through the Language Master, which played the previously recorded words, "Watch me." When he obtained the fire truck, approached a parent, imitated the recording, and activated the truck's siren, his parents responded with language that he could understand, such as "Red fire truck," or "I like fire trucks."

Chapter 1 discussed the importance of including social interaction tasks in activity schedules. There are several ways to accomplish this. Social exchanges, like other activities, can be

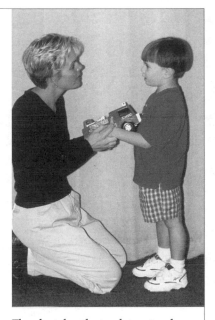

Then he takes the truck to a teacher or parent, says, "Watch me," and activates the truck's siren.

represented by photographs. For example, a picture of a child with one hand raised may cue a greeting, such as waving "Hi"; a picture of a child standing in front of a parent and raising both hands may signal a toss in the air; and a picture of a piggy-back ride may indicate that it is time for the youngster to approach a family member for a ride. With these pictures, children who have not yet acquired speech can participate in social activities.

If your youngster has learned to read some sight words, you may use text to cue social interaction. Words such as "juice" or "tickle" might indicate that the child should approach you and say, "I want juice" or "Tickle, please." Or if reading skills have progressed sufficiently, the schedule may include short sentences, such as "I'm done," "I finished my worksheets," or "Look at my picture."

In our experience, many children who are learning to follow first activity schedules have not yet learned to read, and are just beginning to talk. Although they may imitate a few words, they do not engage in spontaneous speech or initiate social interaction, and these are important goals. For these children, the Language Master is often a useful component of activity schedules.

The Language Master is a tape recorder and player that operates with special cards upon which a strip of audiotape is mounted. A parent or professional uses the Language Master to record a script that the child will say, and when the youngster encounters the Language Master card (or a picture of the card) in her schedule, she is taught to place the card in the slot in the

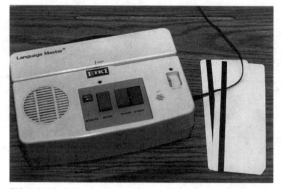

(Fig. 3-7) A Language Master and Language Master cards. See Appendix C for ordering information.

Language Master, listen to the script that is played, and then say the script to a family member or instructor. For example, a child might imitate the script "Look" and show a parent a completed Lego block construction; she might say the script "I love you" and receive a hug from her mother or father; or she might repeat the script, "I did a puzzle." Figure 3-7 shows a Language Master and Language Master cards. Appendix C provides information about how to purchase them.

You can also use a tape recorder to accomplish the same result. Place a picture of the tape recorder in the schedule book, record a brief script, and teach the child to press the "play" button, listen to the script, and press the "stop" button. Use of a tape recorder is a bit more difficult to teach than use of a Language Master, because the child must learn to discriminate "play" and "stop" buttons, and must learn to wait when there are blank spaces on the tape between scripts.

After children become proficient schedule followers, and learn to use the sight words, Language Master cards, or audio tapes included in their schedules, these cues can be faded, so that they can independently initiate conversation and select interaction topics. Procedures for fading written and auditory scripts are explained in more detail in Chapter 10.

If you plan to include the use of the Language Master in your child's schedule, it should be placed on a table, desk, or shelf that is easily within reach, and the previously recorded Language Master card should be mounted in the schedule book or displayed with the other materials included in the activity schedule.

Lawson

A few weeks after we taught Lawson to accept pennies instead of bites of cookie as rewards for good performance, our other daughter, Cecily, complained that her sister was "stealing" pennies from the cup on her dresser. We were delighted, because it was such concrete evidence that Lawson valued the pennies we were giving her for schedule following! (We gave Cecily a new coin purse, and helped her find a place for it in a dresser drawer.)

Lewis

Lewis was barely three when we began his photographic activity schedule. In a curriculum catalog, we found some divided wood shelves with heavy-duty plastic containers that fit into each cubby hole. We thought it would be the perfect way to teach him to put his toys away. But he was so small that when he removed a bin from the shelf, he usually dropped it, spilling the contents. He wasn't tall enough to see into the bins, so he made a lot of errors. And when he put the wood puzzle back in the container and attempted to lift it, he often toppled over head first because of its weight. We moved that bookcase to his brother's room, and bought shelving that was lower, and clear plastic bins that were lighter and easier for Lewis to manage. Teaching went much faster after the change in bookcases.

Ross

Ross already knew how to vacuum the living room, but he never helped out unless we asked, so we took a picture of him in the living room, holding the handle of the vacuum, and added it to his activity schedule. Every time he turned the page and looked at the picture, he went straight to the candy dish on the coffee table, and we always had to guide him back to his schedule. One evening, while we were discussing his progress, we flipped through his schedule book, and suddenly we both noticed that, in the dark background of the photograph, we could see the candy dish. For Ross, that was the most important part of that picture. We took a new photo the next day, hanging a white sheet behind Ross to achieve a plain background. It took several weeks of teaching to help him avoid this error, because he had practiced it so many times.

4 | A Different Way to Teach

It isn't customary to manually guide children through activities, and it looks a bit strange. Why do we recommend such an unusual teaching procedure? The answer is related to prompts.

Prompts are instructions, gestures, demonstrations, touches, or other things that we arrange or do to increase the likelihood that children will make correct responses. Lovaas (1977) defined a prompt as an event that "cues the desired response prior to training or with minimal training" (p. 20). For example, the teacher says, "Stand up," and if the learner does not stand up, the adult lifts him to a standing position. Of course, our goal is to remove prompts as soon as possible, so that children can make correct responses without our help.

In discrete-trial language training, we often prompt children by telling them what to say ("What's this? Say 'apple.'"). Typically, in discrete-trial teaching, the adult gives an instruction or asks a question, the child responds, the adult delivers a reward, the child eats the snack or plays with the toy, and then waits for the next trial to begin. The child's responses are: wait, respond, and use or consume a reward. Thus, passive waiting is one of the responses that is repeatedly rewarded (McClannahan & Krantz, 1997). This may explain why many children with autism who have learned to talk and to do many useful activities do not speak or engage in familiar tasks unless instructed to do so. This is one of the problems that we address when we teach youngsters to follow activity schedules—we teach them to initiate and complete activities and go on to the next activities without waiting for someone to give them directions.

The procedure for teaching activity schedules differs from regular education in another way as well. Teachers of normally developing children usually use a sequence of least-to-most prompts. The teacher asks a question ("Where is your clavicle?") and if the student does not respond, or responds incorrectly, she may model a correct response ("Watch me point to my clavicle"). If the student still does not make a correct response, the teacher may then guide his hand toward his shoulder, and she may even tell him the answer ("Your collar bone is your clavicle").

Although the least-to-most prompts sequence may be successful for typically developing children, it is often ineffective for children with autism, because it permits them to make many errors. After errors occur, they are likely to be repeated, and it becomes increasingly difficult to help a child avoid them. In addition, because we do not deliver rewards for incorrect performances, the child may become inattentive or disruptive.

Why Manual Guidance?

In contrast to the instructional procedures discussed above, the procedure used to teach activity schedules is a most-to-least prompts sequence with manual guidance. We begin with full manual guidance, in order to prevent errors, and we gradually decrease guidance as the child learns the correct responses. The careful reduction of physical guidance is called graduated guidance. Then we move to spatial fading, shadowing, and decreasing our physical proximity, which are discussed later in this chapter. These procedures promote independence and enable young people with autism to complete activities without immediate supervision.

Preparing to Teach

Before the first teaching session, arrange the materials. Place the photographic activity schedule on the far left of the work sur-

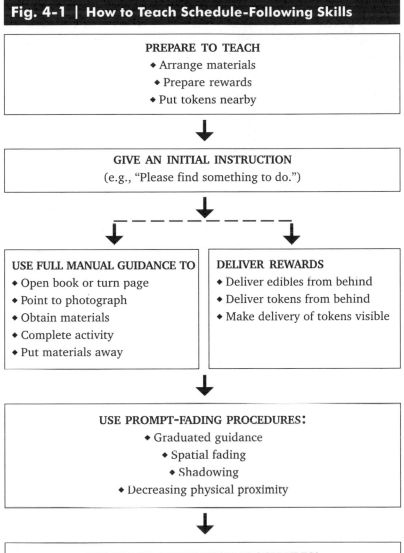

Fig. 4-1 | How to Teach Schedule-Following Skills

PREPARE TO TEACH
- Arrange materials
- Prepare rewards
- Put tokens nearby

GIVE AN INITIAL INSTRUCTION
(e.g., "Please find something to do.")

USE FULL MANUAL GUIDANCE TO
- Open book or turn page
- Point to photograph
- Obtain materials
- Complete activity
- Put materials away

DELIVER REWARDS
- Deliver edibles from behind
- Deliver tokens from behind
- Make delivery of tokens visible

USE PROMPT-FADING PROCEDURES:
- Graduated guidance
- Spatial fading
- Shadowing
- Decreasing physical proximity

USE ERROR-CORRECTION PROCEDURES:
- Return to previous prompt-fading procedure
- Close the schedule book and begin the session again
- Start over; Return to manual guidance and re-teach the entire schedule
- Re-evaluate the power of the rewards
- Substitute a new activity for one that produces many errors

face, and then sequence the materials on the work surface, or on nearby shelves, from left to right, in the order that they will be used. If you want your child to work or play at a desk or table, locate it nearby. If he will play on the floor, be sure that there is an open, uncluttered area adjacent to the target materials. Arrange the available space so that the schedule book will always be clearly visible.

If you will use snacks as rewards (for example, bites of cheese, pieces of apple or cookie, grapes, or cereal), put these in a container that will be easy for you to reach. Do not use large bites or snacks that are not quickly consumed (such as caramels, gummy bears, or hard candy) or you may find that your youngster is still enjoying his reward while making an error. If your child has learned to use a token system, place it near him on the work surface.

It will be helpful if you can avoid answering the door or the telephone or carrying on conversations with family members or colleagues during teaching sessions, but don't worry about noise from the television, the sounds of siblings or other students at play, or the occasional entry or exit of another family member or therapist. Youngsters must learn to engage in activities when distractions are present.

The Initial Instruction

When you are ready to begin the teaching session, give the child one initial instruction, such as "Play with your toys," "Find something to do," or "It's time to do your after-school jobs." Select a direction that is quite general, and that will be comfortable and appropriate even after he or she is a proficient schedule follower. You may want to select an instruction that you give to your other children, such as "Go play," or "Please get busy."

Give the initial instruction only once. After you have given it, do not talk to your child again until he turns to a picture that indicates that he should interact with you, or until he has completed his schedule. Remember, you are teaching independence from adult instructions.

Manual Guidance

After giving the initial instruction, step behind your child and guide her to her activity schedule. This is typically accomplished by holding her shoulders or upper arms and moving her toward the schedule. Putting your hands over her hands, help her open the schedule book and point to the first picture. Then guide her to the target materials, and guide her to pick them up and deposit them on the floor or on a nearby work surface.

Next, guide her to complete the task depicted in her schedule book. If it is a familiar task (such as completing a frame-tray puzzle) provide only the amount of guidance needed to prevent errors. When the puzzle is completed, guide her to pick it up and return it to its position on the shelf or work surface. Then guide her back to the schedule, guide her to turn the page, point to the next picture, obtain the relevant materials, take them to the desk or floor, and complete that task.

Repeat this procedure for every activity in the photographic schedule. Manually guide your child to: open the schedule book or turn a page; point to a photograph; obtain the depicted materials and take them to the work area; complete the task; return the materials to their original location; and return to the schedule and turn a page.

Parents and teachers frequently report that the most difficult aspect of this teaching procedure is remembering not to talk to the child. Remind yourself that your verbal instructions may become embedded in the activities, preventing your son or daughter or student from achieving independence.

Delivering Rewards

When you begin to teach schedule following, deliver rewards frequently. If you are using snack foods as rewards, deliver them from behind your child. If he is cooperative and working well, reach around and place a bit of snack food in his mouth. Try to time the delivery of the reward so that it occurs simultaneously with his appropriate behavior. Do this as frequently as possible, but don't reward him if he is delaying, making an error, resisting your guidance, or engaging in tantrum behavior or stereotypy.

Children who have learned to use token systems do not need immediate food rewards. If you are using a token system, give pennies, stickers, or happy faces often, and attempt to deliver them in such a way that the youngster will notice them. When he is using his schedule, or obtaining or putting away materials, the token board should be nearby on the work surface, where he can easily see the delivery of tokens. When he is playing on the floor or completing an activity at a desk, move the token board to that location, but remember to deliver tokens from behind, not from in front, and to deliver them only when he is working appropriately. In mentoring new teachers and therapists, we have noticed that it is helpful to remind them that the behavior a child is displaying when a reward is delivered is a behavior that is likely to increase in frequency. If we reward children at the moment that they are pointing to pictures in their schedules, they will be more likely to point to the pictures. If we reward them at the moment that they are pausing and doing nothing, such delays will be more frequent. Don't reward behavior that you don't want your child to repeat.

Many children who embark on first activity schedules have begun to use token systems, but earn only four or five tokens before these are exchanged for a preferred food or activity. With these children, pennies or stickers should be augmented by tangible rewards. For example, you might give your child bites of a snack while he points to a picture and obtains and completes the depicted activity, but give him a token when he puts the materials away. Timing the delivery of the last token with the last activity (such as a special snack) may increase the value of the tokens. Remember that the tokens are exchanged for an additional reward (a special toy, snack, tickle, or play activity, accompanied by your praise and attention).

Some Do's and Don'ts

We have already mentioned one "don't"—don't talk to your youngster while he is learning to follow his schedule, unless the schedule dictates a social activity. You have selected some activities that you want him to do all by himself; help him by curtailing your talk, so that he won't be dependent on your instructions.

Another don't—don't gesture. Ultimately, your child will own his schedule, and will select, sequence, and complete activities on his own. But if your gestures become relevant cues, he won't achieve this level of independence. When in doubt, guide him from behind, but don't point to his schedule book or toys.

When we train novice teachers and therapists, we often tell them, "Stay out of the way." That is, don't place any part of your body between the child and his schedule or materials. The presence of clothing and a picture of clothing in an activity schedule should evoke dressing; an available computer and a picture of a computer in an activity schedule should result in keyboarding; a

Fig. 4-2 | Some Do's and Don'ts about Teaching

DO	DON'T
Display materials on shelf or bookcase	Attempt to teach a first schedule in a cluttered or disorganized environment
Arrange not to answer door or phone	Worry about noise from TV or other children
Arrange materials in sequence	Get between the child and the materials
Prepare rewards in advance	Use these rewards at other times
Give one initial instruction	Talk, except during social activities
Use manual guidance, and guide quickly to prevent errors or delays	Point, gesture, model, or reach in front of the child
Deliver rewards frequently	Deliver rewards when the child is delaying or behaving inappropriately

food preparation task and a picture of hands under the faucet should result in handwashing. Standing between a child and his materials, or reaching in front of rather than behind him, may delay his learning to complete a task independently.

On the other hand, you can make some critical decisions that will promote independence. If a child begins to engage in stereotypic or disruptive behavior, quickly guide him to do the scheduled activity. If he delays in pointing to a picture, obtaining materials, or completing the activity, use manual guidance before he makes an incorrect or inappropriate response. If he cries, verbally objects, or attempts to stop the activity, guide him to continue. Figure 4-2 summarizes some of the do's and don'ts.

Graduated Guidance

As noted above, teaching begins with full, hand-over-hand manual guidance. But after a few sessions, you will notice that your child is becoming less dependent upon your guidance. You may feel him move his arm to turn a page, or feel him turn toward the bookshelf, or reach to pick up Lego blocks and put them back in the basket without depending on your help. Try lightly resting your hands on his without guiding. His responses will let you know how much guidance is necessary. For example, if he puts the pieces in the puzzle without your guidance, don't continue to guide. But do use guidance to prevent errors. If you feel his arms reaching for a toy that does not correspond to the photograph in his schedule, immediately guide his hands to the correct toy. If he often attempts to put beads in his mouth, prevent this behavior by guiding him to string the beads.

Typically children master some tasks quickly, and others more slowly. Some youngsters need sustained manual guidance in order to learn to turn pages; others need continuing guidance to learn to return materials to their original locations on the shelves; still others need ongoing guidance to learn to run cards through the Language Master. By carefully attending to your child's movements, you will learn which responses to guide and which responses no longer require your guidance. If you are merely covering his hands with yours while he does the target activity, you are ready to move to spatial fading.

Spatial Fading

Spatial fading means gradually changing the location of manual prompts (Cooper, 1987). If a youngster systematically points to pictures in her schedule, her teacher may stop using hand-over-hand prompts for these tasks, and may now lightly hold her wrist. If she continues to point to the pictures, the teacher may lightly hold her forearm, and later, her upper arm and then her elbow. And if correct responding continues, the teacher may eventually only touch her shoulder when she points.

The skillful use of these teaching procedures depends upon careful observation of a child's behavior. When teaching a first schedule, you will no doubt find that you must continue to use graduated guidance for some responses, but that you can use spatial fading for others. Waiting too long to fade prompts slows children's progress, but fading prompts too soon results in errors that also impede learning. You will learn from your child when to fade.

Shadowing

If your child performs the desired behavior when you are merely touching his shoulder, you may begin to shadow him. Shadowing means that you follow his movements very closely with your hands, but without touching him (Cooper, 1987), and if he continues to display correct responses, you gradually move your hands farther away from him.

When Owen was learning to follow his first schedule, we found that he, like most other children with autism, required a combination of graduated guidance, spatial fading, and shadowing. He quickly learned to obtain materials and we were soon shadowing these responses, with the exception that he often attempted to have his snack before opening the schedule book; we continued graduated guidance in order to prevent this error. While manually guiding to prevent him from throwing the stacking cups, we used spatial fading to help him put the shapes in the shape box. Although he learned to complete some tasks more quickly than others, he eventually completed all of them with shadowing, and it was time to increase the distance between him and his teacher.

Decreasing Physical Proximity

When your youngster correctly completes all of the components of the activity schedule with shadowing, take the final prompt-fading step—fade your presence. Initially you may step back and increase the distance between you and your child by six inches. In the next session, if correct responses continue, you may stand one foot away. Like other decisions about prompt fading, decisions about decreasing proximity are based upon your child's performance. If he continues to make correct responses in the next sessions, move one foot away, then two feet away, and so on.

When group home therapists shadowed him, Al, age 10, correctly completed a morning activity schedule that included photographs of getting dressed and making his bed. Next they decreased their distance in six-inch increments. When they were one foot away and he completed the target activities without errors, they moved eighteen inches away, then two feet away, and so on. Eventually, they stood outside his bedroom door, and then moved around the corner and out of sight.

Dealing with Errors

All children make errors when learning to follow activity schedules. Initially they do not know what is expected of them.

In addition, most have previously learned some behaviors that are incompatible with schedule following, such as waiting for an adult to give an instruction or provide play materials; helping themselves to snacks that are now included in the schedule; flipping, rather than turning pages of books; or spinning toys, rather than using them for their intended purposes.

The most-to-least prompts sequence, discussed earlier, is designed to prevent errors whenever possible, but even the most expert clinicians are sometimes unable to do this. Occasionally, a child moves with surprising speed, engages in a completely unexpected behavior, successfully evades manual guidance, engages in disruptive behavior, or appears to be making a correct response that, at the last moment, is transformed into an error.

The strategy for dealing with errors is: Return to the previous prompting procedure. If you are shadowing a child who makes an error, return to spatial fading. If you are using spatial fading, return to graduated guidance. And if you are using graduated guidance, return to full, hand-over-hand manual guidance. Continue to use the previous prompting procedure until the youngster has made one or more correct responses on the schedule component associated with the error; then again fade prompts. For example, if the child attempts to move on to the next part of the schedule before putting materials away, return to the previous prompting procedure until he has correctly returned one or two bins to the shelf. If this error occurs near the end of the schedule, it may be necessary to use the prior prompting procedure in the next session.

If you are using graduated guidance and your son tries to obtain materials before turning the page and pointing to the picture of those materials, use full manual guidance to help him turn the page and point to the picture. Continue to use full guidance on the next several opportunities to turn a page and point to the picture, and then return to graduated guidance. If you are shadowing your daughter as she puts a piece in a puzzle, and she attempts to put the puzzle away before completing it, return to spatial fading, but if another error occurs, return to graduated guidance.

Repeated errors indicate that a child has not yet really learned the tasks, or has not yet learned to benefit from the prompting procedures. Under these circumstances, you may consider several alternatives. One of these is to start over—to reteach the entire schedule, beginning again with hand-over-hand guidance. Another option is to respond to errors by closing the schedule book, returning materials to their original locations, and guiding your child to begin the session again. However, don't require him to do one particular activity several times—he may learn that this task is to be completed more than once.

You may also want to reconsider the available rewards. Are there other snacks or toys that your child prefers? Are rewards delivered frequently? And you may want to reassess the activities in the schedule. Is a particular activity always associated with errors? For example, does your youngster typically make errors on a color-sorting task, or on a tracing worksheet? Does she usually line up the Lego blocks, rather than building with them? If one activity usually produces errors, it can be removed and replaced by a different photograph and different materials.

Finally, it may be important to evaluate your child's responses to manual guidance. If he regularly tantrums or resists, it may be necessary to temporarily discontinue the activity schedule, and return to the procedures for teaching him to accept touching and guidance (see Chapter 2).

Putting it All Together

By now, you may be wondering how to do so many things simultaneously (see Figure 4-1 for a flow chart of all of these tasks). You must manually guide your child; put edible rewards in his mouth (if tokens have not yet acquired sufficient value); deliver tokens in such a way that he notices that he has earned a penny or sticker; remember which of his responses require graduated guidance, spatial fading, or shadowing; and be prepared to use an error-correction procedure.

Typically we learn this complex repertoire through practice, and through feedback from others. Your child's successes and errors may teach you how to change your behavior in the next session. And if you and your spouse are jointly undertaking this project, you may help one another by observing and commenting on the effective use of the teaching procedures, and on occasions when the teaching procedures were not followed, or were followed inconsistently. Your partner, like your youngster, will be more responsive if rewards are more frequent than correction.

Occasionally both parents and professionals observe that they have inadvertently taught incorrect responses. When this happens, we can take comfort in the scientific knowledge that children's behavior is pliable and responsive to the environment. By changing the teaching procedures, enhancing the rewards, or altering photographs or materials, we can correct errors and help children achieve important next steps.

5 | Measuring Schedule-Following

Introduction

Although collecting data is a critical part of teaching a child to use an activity schedule, some parents and teachers are uninterested in it. Teaching a child to follow a schedule requires that you attend to a plethora of details. And when he independently follows the schedule, his new skills will be obvious to you and others. Thus, you may wonder why you should bother with data collection.

There are several answers to this question. First, data on your son's performance will help to identify tasks that are often associated with errors, so that you can be prepared to use the error-correction procedures described in the previous chapter. Second, the data will help you make decisions about when to fade prompts. And finally, the data will reveal when it is time to introduce variations in the schedule, or introduce a new schedule. Although Kip's parents reported that he had mastered his first schedule, data collected by his instructor indicated that he was correctly completing 68% to 74% of schedule components. Casual observation is not always accurate; in Kip's case, the data showed that he needed continued teaching in order to achieve success.

Collecting Data

Gathering data on a child's use of her schedule isn't really daunting, and it gives us a detailed picture of performance. It allows us to examine many separate responses, and makes it possible to determine which parts of a task are difficult, so that we can be prepared to provide instruction exactly when it is most needed. In order to get this fine-grained analysis of a youngster's schedule-following skills, we break each task into several separate components.

Most activities in the schedule have five components: 1) opening the schedule book or turning a page; 2) looking at and pointing to a picture; 3) obtaining the depicted materials; 4) completing the activity; and 5) putting the materials away. Correct responses are scored plus (+) and incorrect responses are scored minus (-). Before you begin to teach, write the activities in the left column of the data sheet, in the order that they appear in the schedule, and put the data sheet on a clipboard (see Appendix B for a blank data sheet).

Suppose that you are teaching a preschooler to use a six-page schedule book; the photographs included in the book show a puzzle, a shape box, the youngster being tickled, a Potato Head toy, a color matching task, and raisins on a plate. The first component of the puzzle activity is scored as correct if the youngster opens her schedule book to the first page without any help (see Figure 5-1). The second component, pointing to and looking at the picture, is scored as correct only if she points and looks. Because you are standing behind her, you can't see her eyes, but consider that she is looking if her head is oriented toward the picture. If she is turned away from the picture, gently guide her head to help her orient, and score this component incorrect.

The third component, obtaining materials, is scored as correct if she moves from the schedule to the puzzle or puzzle container, picks it up, and takes it to the work surface or floor. The fourth component, completing the activity, is scored as correct if she puts all of the pieces in the puzzle (and returns the puzzle to the container, if you have provided one). And the fifth component is scored as correct if she returns the puzzle (or puzzle in container) to its original location on the shelf or bookcase.

Each component is scored as correct only if the child completes it without any help from you. That is, you do not touch her, talk to her, gesture to materials, or do anything else that may assist

Fig. 5-1 | Data sheet

Sample data sheet used to measure a child's acquisition of schedule-following skills. (Blank data sheet found in Appendix B.)

Activity	Opens Book/ Turns Page	Points/ Looks	Obtains	Completes	Puts Away
OBSERVER: Dad					
DATE: Dec. 20, 1998					
Puzzle	-	+	-	-	-
Shape Box	-	-	+	+	-
Ask for Tickle	+	-	N/A	+	N/A
Potato Head	-	-	-	-	-
Color Matching	-	+	-	+	-
Snack	-	+	-	+	-
# Completed	1	3	1	4	0
Number of components correctly completed: 9					
Total number of components: 28					
Percentage of components correctly completed: 32%					

her in making a correct response. If you provide help of any kind, score that component incorrect. In addition, if she pauses or delays for more than 10 seconds, or engages in inappropriate behavior, score the component incorrect and prompt a correct response.

Although most activities in the schedule have five components, a few have less than five; often, social interactions have only three. The schedule shown in Figure 5-1 includes asking for a tickle. The child's tasks are: turn the page, look at and point to the picture of being tickled, and go to someone and say "Tickle, please." There are no materials to obtain or put away, and these activity components are scored "NA" (not applicable).

The data sheet in Figure 5-1 shows that the youngster did not independently turn the page to the color-matching picture, and this was scored minus. However, after being helped to turn the page, she did point to and look at the picture of the color-matching materials, and her parent marked a plus for that task component. She needed help in obtaining the color-matching bin, and minus was scored. Although she correctly completed the color-matching task by sticking the red circle on the corresponding red circle, the yellow circle on the yellow circle, and so on, she did not put the materials away until she was prompted to do so, and "puts away" was scored minus.

Having a snack is the final activity shown in Figure 5-1. The schedule included a picture of raisins on a paper plate, and the plate of raisins was displayed on a shelf. The child ate some of the raisins without prompts (her parents did not require that she eat them all), and the activity was scored as correctly completed. She did not put the paper plate in the wastebasket without help, and "putting away" was scored as incorrect.

After a teaching session, add the pluses in each column of the data sheet and enter the totals in the bottom row. This is a good time to review each task component and plan prompting and prompt-fading strategies for the next session.

Next, summarize the data by filling in the blanks at the bottom of the data sheet. Count the total number of components correctly completed, and the total number of components in the schedule. Then divide the number correct by the total number of components and multiply by 100 to obtain the percentage of components correctly completed. In Figure 5-1, nine of twenty-eight schedule components were scored as correctly completed. The youngster's parents divided 9 by 28 and then multiplied by 100 to obtain the percentage correct (32%). Later in this chapter, we explain how to use this percentage to create a graph that displays a youngster's acquisition of schedule-following skills.

Solving Data-Collection Problems

Often one parent teaches schedule following while the other is at work, commuting, attending to other children, preparing meals, shopping, or doing other essential tasks. How can you collect data on your son's performance while using manual guidance and delivering snacks and tokens? The use of a tape recorder is one solution. Turn the recorder on and place it nearby before beginning the session, and record your narration of the outcome of each task component. For example, "Potato Head. Turns page, plus. Points and looks, minus." At a less busy time, you can transcribe this information onto the data sheet.

Some parents invite another child in the family to assist with data collection. Teenagers, and even younger children, may enjoy observing sessions and recording the symbols that you dictate. If you enlist a child's help, teach him or her to stay nearby, and to hold the data sheet where you can see it, so that you can verify correct scoring and indicate when corrections are needed.

Attempting to memorize the data and record them after the session ends is not a good solution to data-collection problems. Few of us can accurately recall twenty or more separate responses and whether they were prompted or unprompted. If you cannot use a tape recorder or enlist the help of your spouse or another child, you may want to withdraw your prompts for a few seconds, or use manual guidance to stop the activity for a few seconds, while you quickly record a plus or minus. Data collection will become much easier as you practice, and as your youngster acquires skills. When you begin to use shadowing, and when you later decrease your proximity, you'll have much more time to record data.

Occasionally you and your partner may be able to collect data at the same time. This exercise can be especially useful if, after the session, you compare your data sheets and talk about agreements and disagreements. These discussions often reveal error patterns or unintended prompts that were not obvious to the person who delivered instruction.

Graphing the Data

A graph gives you a session-to-session, week-to-week, and month-to-month overview of a youngster's acquisition of schedule-following skills. Although you may want to keep and periodically review the data sheets in order to look for error patterns, they will be less helpful than graphs in tracking a child's overall progress.

On graph paper divided by tens, number the left side of the graph from ten to one hundred, and label it "Percentage of components correctly completed." Label the bottom of the graph "Sessions," and add a date each time you graph another session. If

Fig. 5-2 | Photographic Activity Schedule
A first photographic activity schedule for Brice, age 3.

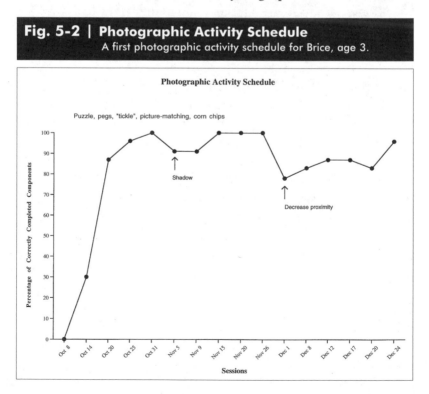

Photographic Activity Schedule

Puzzle, pegs, "tickle", picture-matching, corn chips

Shadow

Decrease proximity

Percentage of Correctly Completed Components

Sessions

you conduct more than one session per day, you may want to indicate both date and time. At the top of the page, you may add information that will be useful in making later comparisons. For example, "Schedule 1: Puzzle, Pegs, Tickle, Picture Matching, and Corn Chips" (see Figure 5-2).

After each session, add a data point; if the child scored 30% correct, plot 30% on the graph. Experienced clinicians know that graphing is relatively effortless if it is accomplished each day, but becomes drudgery if ungraphed data accumulate. In addition, each day's data point is a bit of information that may be useful in planning the next day's teaching. You can use arrows on graphs to highlight noteworthy events, such as the beginning of shadowing or decreasing proximity (Figure 5-2). You can also use arrows to indicate other changes, such as replacing a photograph or an activity that produced many errors.

One of the most important things to do with a graph is to display it. Show your graph to your son's grandparents, aunts and uncles, and teachers; show it to family friends, and discuss his progress. Just as he needs rewards for learning to follow his schedule, you also need rewards for your hard work in helping him acquire these important skills.

6 | The First Schedule is Mastered!

Introduction

After several consecutive sessions in which a boy or girl scores 80% to 100% correct, while you are standing eight or ten feet away, you may consider the first schedule mastered. Don't wait too long to take the next steps (described below)—the youngster's performance may decline if the same tasks are presented again and again in the same order.

New Activity Sequences

Becoming a schedule follower does not mean learning a specific chain of responses. To be truly independent, children must become "picture readers"—they must learn to do any activity represented by a picture in a schedule book. Changing the order of pictures teaches them to attend to and to act on cues in the schedule.

Perry was seven when he began his first schedule, which included the following sequence of activities: putting twenty-five pieces in their correct places in the shape-matching game, Perfection; drawing a picture, using a stencil and crayon; asking a parent for a "high five"; sorting pictures of food and clothing into separate containers; and having a snack (popcorn) and putting the paper plate in a nearby wastebasket.

After he learned to complete these activities while a parent stood in the doorway of his room and did not prompt, the photographs in his schedule were rearranged. The picture of the Perfection game continued to be first, because his parents were concerned that he would not begin the schedule if a different picture appeared on page one. The picture of popcorn remained on the last page, as a reward for completing the scheduled activities. The other three pictures in his schedule book were placed in a new order—sorting, stencil, and "high five." To help him master the new activity sequence, the materials on his shelves were also rearranged, so that the order of the materials matched the order of photographs in his schedule.

On the first teaching session after the photographs were rearranged, Perry independently began his schedule as usual, and completed the Perfection game activity without prompts. Upon turning to the second page and encountering a different photograph, he stopped for a few seconds, and then rapidly turned pages. At this point, his father quickly stepped forward and manually guided him to point to the picture on page two, obtain the sorting materials, and begin the task. After this prompt to begin, Perry independently completed the sorting activity, put the materials away, returned to his schedule, turned the page, and again encountered a photograph in a new position. He scrutinized the picture of the crayon and stencil for a full ten seconds, but when his father stepped forward to provide manual guidance, he turned and obtained the materials without help, completed the activity, and put the materials back on the shelf (because his father prompted him by increasing his proximity, he scored "obtains" as incorrect).

Upon returning to the schedule, turning the page, and again finding a photograph in a new order, Perry darted toward the snack. His father, who had been shadowing, intercepted him, guided him back to the book, and used hand-over-hand guidance to help him point to the picture of "high five." Because Perry vocally objected and engaged in stereotypic arm tensing and finger play, he was guided to give a "high five" (his father participated in this social activity by saying, "Yeah, Little Guy"), after which he independently walked back to the book, pointed to the picture of the snack, ate the popcorn, threw away the paper plate, and was rewarded with a roughhousing and tickling game known to his family as "sack the quarterback."

In subsequent sessions, Perry's performance was variable, and his parents continued to shadow him, occasionally providing manual guidance or spatial fading to prevent errors. He began the fifth session by opening the book and examining all of the pages before turning back to page one and pointing to the first picture. Because his perusal was completed in less than ten seconds, he was not prompted. His parents interpreted this as an exploratory response—he appeared to be reviewing the new sequence of photographs.

When Perry's pictures and activities were resequenced, his parents drew a horizontal, dotted line on the graph, and labeled

Fig. 6-1 | Photographic Activity Schedule
A first photographic activity schedule for Perry, age 7.

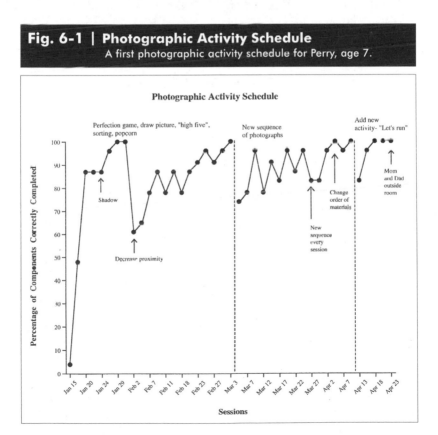

it "New Sequence of Photographs" (see Figure 6-1). When his performance stabilized—he correctly completed 80% to 100% of schedule components without prompts in five consecutive sessions—his mom and dad provided a different sequence of photographs in *each* session and, later, they placed materials on the shelves in an order that did not match the order of pictures in the schedule (see arrows, Figure 6-1). At this time, Perry's parents noted that when they were in his room, he often took their hands and pulled them toward his schedule book, or independently picked it up, opened it, and began to do depicted activities.

Perry's story offers a good example of how to resequence photographs and activities. First, change the order of a few pictures in the schedule, and change the arrangement of materials to match the new picture sequence. Then teach the new sequence until it is mastered. Secondly, rearrange photographs every session, and change the order of all of the pictures. And finally, after performance stabilizes, rearrange materials so that they are no longer presented in an order that matches the sequence of pictures in the schedule book.

New Pictures and Activities

When a child has learned to follow a schedule in which pictures and activities are regularly resequenced, it is time to add a new photograph and activity to his first schedule. You can facilitate the youngster's acquisition if you select an activity that is both familiar and preferred. For example, if the last picture in the schedule shows potato chips, you may decide to move this photo to a middle page, and add a new last page that depicts a different but equally rewarding activity, such as juice, a swing in the air, a ride in the wagon, or an opportunity to watch part of a favorite video.

When the new activity is added, be prepared to return to hand-over-hand guidance to help the youngster master the expanded schedule, and use the prompt-fading procedures discussed in Chapter 4 (graduated guidance, spatial fading, shadowing, and decreasing proximity). Perry's parents added his popcorn snack to the first half of his schedule, and added a new, familiar activity, requesting a run around the recreation room, as the sixth and last activity (see Figure 6-1).

After the first new activity is mastered add a second new photo to the schedule book, but retain an especially enjoyable activity as the last activity. As in the previous examples, assist your child by selecting a familiar task. Perry's parents added a Lincoln Logs fort as a second new activity; he had previously built the fort with assistance. The photograph in his schedule showed the completed structure, and prompts and prompt-fading procedures enabled him to independently assemble it.

Continue to add new pictures and activities to the schedule, but fit the schedule to your child's capabilities. A preschooler may learn to complete a series of activities that takes about fifteen minutes, but an eight-year-old may engage in scheduled activities for thirty minutes or more.

New Independence

If a youngster completes scheduled activities without assistance when photographs are regularly resequenced, when two or three new activities have been added, and when the materials are frequently rearranged, it's time to emphasize independence. Return to the procedures detailed in Chapter 4 to decrease your proximity, but continue until you are outside the room and no longer in sight.

Initially you will want to peek in about every 15 seconds, and if your son is not following the schedule, return to the prior prompting procedure (shadowing). But again fade your presence as soon as his performance is stable. If you observe that he is dependably following the schedule, gradually increase the time between observations. Check on him every 30 seconds, then every minute, then every 2 minutes, and so on, until you are doing only a few random, unpredictable observations.

If you have been delivering tokens for schedule following, you will want to decrease the frequency of token delivery at the same time that you fade your presence. Instead of giving your youngster one token at a time, give him two or three tokens when you make occasional checks, provide the last tokens after he has finished the schedule, and exchange the tokens for the special activity.

At this point, you will have created a ten- to thirty-minute period during which you can turn your attention to other matters, such as finishing the laundry, starting dinner preparation, helping another child with homework, or enjoying a well-deserved coffee break. But at regular intervals—for example, every third session, or every fifth session—you'll still want to observe continuously and collect data. The data will alert you to problems that can often be corrected in a few sessions, using the original teaching procedures.

New Problems, Familiar Solutions

The last step in prompt fading—fading the adult's proximity—is often the most difficult; it's not unusual for children to make errors or engage in stereotypy when parents or teachers are no longer in sight. The absence of adults is the ultimate test of whether we have diminished the prompt dependence discussed in Chapter 1.

If returning to the prior prompting procedure does not resolve a child's performance problems, consider some alternate strategies. One of these is to step in when the first error occurs, and use full manual guidance for the remainder of the session. On the next session, resume fading of proximity, but be prepared to return to manual guidance if an error occurs. The data on schedule following will reveal whether this tactic is effective; if it achieves the desired outcome, the youngster's percentage correct will gradually increase over several sessions.

If returning to manual guidance for the remainder of the session does not achieve the desired result, explore another alternative. Step in when the first error occurs, put materials away, close the schedule book, guide the child to start the schedule from the beginning, and use hand-over-hand manual guidance for the entire session. At the next opportunity for schedule following, return to fading your proximity but close the schedule book, start over, and use full manual guidance if an error is again observed.

Another option, which provides children with very clear feedback, is token removal, sometimes called response cost (Lutzker, McGimsey McRae, & McGimsey, 1983, p. 42). Take away a token when the youngster makes an error, and return it when he is performing well. If errors persist over several sessions, take tokens but do not return them, and allow him to learn that if he has not earned all of the tokens, he cannot exchange them for a special activity or treat. You may also decide to use token loss in addition to providing manual guidance (described above).

If none of these strategies is effective, return to the prompts (graduated guidance, spatial fading, shadowing) that enable your child to be successful and repeat the prompt-fading procedures, but this time, fade prompts more slowly. It may be especially important to do more gradual fading of your physical proximity. You might try increasing your distance six inches at a time. Although it may take a considerable amount of time to fade your proximity, remember the importance of this endeavor—it can help your child achieve real independence.

When exploring solutions to new problems, parents and teachers often find it helpful to review their own behavior. Verbal instructions and gestures should not be used to teach schedule-following skills. Prompts should be used to prevent errors whenever possible. When errors are corrected or tokens are removed, the adult should be nonemotional and matter-of-fact. Correct responses should be rewarded immediately with tokens or edibles. And children should receive special attention and preferred activities after completing their schedules.

Finally, regular data-collection and graphing is essential to problem solving. Your data will tell you whether you have helped your child surmount performance problems.

New Schedules

If your child follows a schedule without your help (although you may be just beyond the doorway, or at the other end of a large room), it's time to consider adding a new schedule. But don't abandon the first one—just continue to resequence the pictures and materials.

Occasionally you may also remove a photograph and a corresponding task from the first schedule, and replace an old activity with a new one, to add interest. Over a period of time, the activities you remove can be used to construct a second schedule—one that can be packaged in a book bag or backpack and completed at grandma's house, on a family vacation, or during a time of day that is particularly busy.

In addition to creating a new schedule from old activities, push on to new territory. Your youngster's schedule-following skills will grow as a result of each new schedule that is mastered. As a parent of a child with autism, you are probably very busy and over-committed. This is a good time to consider how the next schedule can make a positive contribution to family life.

If morning is a particularly hectic time, you may want to develop a new schedule that facilitates completion of morning routines. Such a schedule might include pictures that cue a preschooler to put cereal bowl and juice glass on the counter after breakfast, put book bag and coat near the front door, and obtain and use "See 'N' Say" toys until the bus arrives.

For an older child, a morning schedule might include obtaining a glass and bowl, pouring juice and cereal, eating breakfast, putting dishes in the dishwasher, putting a lunch box in a book bag, putting the book bag near the front door, and watching television until the bus arrives. As your child becomes a more proficient schedule follower, you can make decisions about whether to add new activities that are familiar and previously mastered, or activities that your youngster hasn't yet learned to do. If he doesn't yet know how to put his lunch box in his book bag, you'll have to manually guide these responses initially, and later fade your prompts. Although it's a busy time of day, the lunch box has to end up in the book bag, and the morning routine will eventually run more smoothly if your son learns to do these tasks himself.

Some youngsters with autism tantrum when family routines are altered. Consider developing a schedule that will help your girl or boy deal with change. You might begin with a schedule book that includes photographs of a familiar play activity; obtaining hat and coat; saying "Let's go," or taking your hand; walking with you to the mailbox; and returning to the house for a snack. When this schedule is mastered, replace getting the mail with riding a trike, and later, with going to the convenience store, bringing in the garbage cans, transporting a sibling, or picking up a commuting parent at the train or bus station. The goal is to rotate these activities as needed to accommodate family members' schedules.

Initially each new activity schedule will require the same (or almost the same) effort and attention to detail that was necessary to teach the first schedule. But if you are systematic in teaching schedule following, this investment will eventually yield important benefits for your child with autism and other members of your family, and later schedules will be mastered more quickly.

7 | When Do Activities End?

Introduction

The activities discussed in previous chapters all have clear endings. The stacking rings are completed when all rings are on the spindle, a worksheet is finished when each item has been answered, and a social activity is over after the youngster initiates and someone responds. But some activities are of indeterminate length, and many children who are successful schedule-followers have not yet learned to tell time. How long should a child watch television, play with dolls or cars, or play computer games?

Using Timers

Many young people who have learned to follow photographic activity schedules quickly learn to set timers, if we teach these skills within the already-familiar context of schedule following. Setting an inexpensive digital kitchen timer typically requires only a few button presses, and photographs in the youngster's schedule can cue these responses.

Small electronic timers are available in hardware and variety stores. Timers with magnets on the back are particularly convenient, because they can be easily mounted on the clipboard used for delivering tokens. These timers often have buttons of different colors, and it is therefore possible to add pictorial cues to the activity schedule to teach a child to press the buttons in a particular sequence.

Suppose that a five-year-old nonreader enjoys looking at picture books, and we want to add this activity to her schedule. We observe that she often looks at books for three to five minutes before losing interest, and we decide to teach her to set a timer for three minutes. This requires pushing the "clear" button once, pushing the "min" button three times, and pushing the "start" button once.

The activity schedule displays a picture of the timer, which cues her to remove it from her clipboard; next, it highlights the black clear button (which she will press once), three pictures of the white minute button (which she will push three times), and one picture of the red start button (which she will push once). This sequence of pictures is shown in Figure 7-1. If the timer does not have different-colored keys, we can modify it, using small pieces of plastic tape.

The teaching procedures are familiar. When the child first encounters the new pictures in her schedule, we use manual guidance to help her point to a photograph of the timer, pick it up and place it on a work surface; point to the picture of the black key and press that key; point to the picture of the white key and press it; and so on. When the timer rings, we immediately guide her to put the books away, return to the schedule, turn the page, and continue. Just as before, graduated guidance is replaced by spatial fading, shadowing, and then decreasing proximity.

Learning to use timers creates new options for many children. Jerry, age 7, liked to draw, and often drew pictures for extended periods, meanwhile neglecting other tasks. He learned to set a timer for ten minutes and move on to the next activity when drawing time ended. Duncan, age 10, enjoyed playing an electronic keyboard; the timer signaled him when it was time to do something else. Thirteen-year-old Vic was a connoisseur of Star Trek videotapes. Because he had acquired some arithmetic skills, his schedule showed a numeral beside a picture of the minute button, and his parents frequently changed the number of minutes of viewing time, so that Vic's schedule would be compatible with other family members' schedules.

Fig. 7-1 | Pictorial Cues When Using a Timer

Pictorial cues used to help a child learn to set a timer. Initially, each picture appears on a separate page of the schedule book.

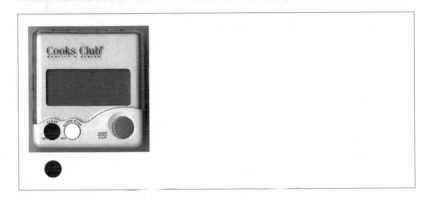

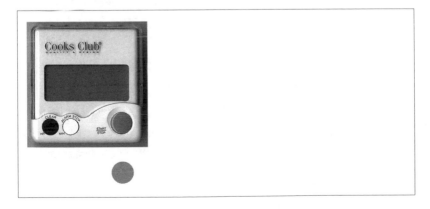

After learning to use timers, many children (including those without math skills) begin to "cheat." They set the timer for less than the specified amount of time when doing less-preferred activities, and for more time when doing favorite activities. "Cheating" often means that it is time to offer choices. Youngsters who read may be ready for a textual cue such as, "Set timer—my choice." Nonreaders may be given similar opportunities by replacing a number in the schedule with a blank space.

Many children with autism engage in repetitive or dysfunctional behavior if an activity lasts too long. When teaching children to make choices about how to allot time, do not use manual guidance if the child sets the timer for an appropriate amount of time, but guide the youngster if he or she attempts to select an amount of time that is much longer or shorter than the desirable duration of a particular activity. For example, if a girl who is about to watch Sesame Street videotapes sets the timer for 15 minutes, you may decide to permit this; if she attempts to set the timer for 50 minutes, you may want to manually guide her to select a shorter period of time.

Although we want young people to learn to make choices about how to use time, we continue to specify the duration of some activities. If the schedule indicates that typing practice should last 10 minutes and your son sets the timer for 5 minutes, use the error-correction procedures discussed in Chapters 4 and 6. Learning to make choices is important, but following parents' and teachers' instructions is equally important!

Other Time-Management Skills

After learning to use a digital timer, a child may quickly learn to set a microwave oven. Many children enjoy activity schedules that teach them to use a microwave oven to make popcorn, or to heat muffins, pretzels, tortillas, or other snacks. In constructing such a schedule, include photographs of each part of the activity—for example, pictures that cue getting the microwave popcorn bag and a bowl from the cupboard, putting popcorn in the oven, pressing the relevant keys on the microwave key pad, removing the popcorn when the timer rings, opening the popcorn bag, and pouring popcorn into a bowl.

Pictures that cue setting the microwave are similar to the pictures used to teach setting a kitchen timer. For example, the schedule might show separate pictures of the microwave key pad that highlight the "time cook," "4," "min," and "start" keys. If the child does not yet read, use plastic tape to color-code the microwave key pad and the pictures in the schedule book, so that he can match the pictures to the key pad.

After learning to use activity schedules and timers, some young people learn more sophisticated food preparation tasks. Patrick learned to make brownies and bake them in an electric oven. His schedule displayed all of the relevant steps, including setting the correct oven temperature and putting on arm-length oven mitts before using the oven. Because it was difficult for him to determine when the dough was adequately mixed, he set a kitchen timer for 3 minutes, and continued to stir for that period of time. After putting the brownies in the oven, his schedule cued him to set the timer again and clip it to his belt; when the alarm sounded, he returned to the kitchen and removed the brownies from the oven.

Walt, age 16, used a photographic schedule to make a meatloaf dinner. Initially, using the activity schedule, he learned to make only the meatloaf. After this was mastered, his schedule was expanded to include making a salad, then preparing a frozen vegetable, and finally, warming dinner rolls. Subsequently he learned to make a spaghetti dinner, and his food preparation skills continue to expand.

Time-Management Skills and Family Life

After your child learns to use timers, consider how these skills may contribute to your family's routines. If there is a safe outdoor area for jogging, biking, or shooting baskets, you may decide to include time in your child's schedule for these activities. If you are computer users, include time for playing computer games (with manual guidance, many youngsters readily learn to use a mouse, and to open and close preferred programs). If your son is a "couch potato," use his schedule to establish times for watching television. If your daughter resists getting out of the tub, use a timer to establish a predictable end of bathtime as part of a going-to-bed or bathtime activity schedule.

Don't forget to teach your child to set timers for varying amounts of time. At grandma's house, there may be more time for watching television. If company is expected, both computer use and bath time may need to be abbreviated. If we frequently allocate different amounts of time for the activities in children's schedules, they are less likely to resist schedule changes that must be made because of family commitments or unexpected events.

8 | Increasing Choice

Introduction

Dealing with unstructured time is difficult for many young people with autism. When parents or instructors do not provide activities, some youngsters do nothing at all, and others display disruptive or stereotypic behavior. Teaching your child to make choices among activities is an important step toward helping him or her to learn to make productive use of time, and photographic activity schedules can help.

Teaching Children to Choose Rewards

Almost all youngsters can learn to make choices if we provide an appropriate program of instruction. Your child's initial schedules included pictures of preferred snacks, toys, or activities, such as a cup of yogurt, a piggy-back ride, a drink of juice, or blowing bubbles. The next task is to teach him to choose one of two rewards.

Display the photographs that represent available choices on a large foam board or bulletin board. Select two familiar pictures of "special" or preferred activities, place these photographs in baseball card holders, attach them to the board with Velcro, and place this "choice board" on a shelf or work surface that is easily seen by your youngster. When he was a preschooler, the first two photographs mounted on Tod's choice board were Cheerios and a rocking horse.

The next step is to add a blank page to your child's activity schedule book (this page displays only a Velcro dot).Then invite your boy to follow his schedule as usual, but be prepared to prompt. When he turns to the blank page, manually guide him to point to the Velcro dot, go to the choice board, select one of the two photographs, mount it in his schedule book, and then do the activity he selected. As he learns to do this sequence, use the previously described prompt-fading procedures.

After your son has learned to choose one of two activities from the choice board, add a third picture, then a fourth, and so on. When he has learned to select from a field of three to five photographs that depict activity choices, add a second blank page to his schedule.

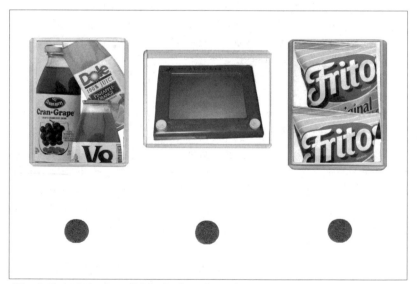

(Fig. 8-1) A choice board that displays three choices.

Over time, continue to add new pictures to the choice board that show other special snacks, toys, or social games that your son enjoys. As the choices expand, you may decide to rotate the pictures on a daily basis. Removing some pictures and adding others makes the choice board more interesting. And don't forget to continue your son's token system—give him coins for making choices, as well as for following the other parts of his schedule. After he finishes his schedule, help him exchange his tokens for an extra-special activity.

Sherman

When he was 32 months old, Sherman mastered his first schedule, which included five photographs. Pictures were resequenced, new pictures were added, and then a choice was introduced. He had recently conquered a variety of matching tasks, and often took our hands and pulled us toward those materials, so we included a shape-matching task as one of his choices. The other choice was a favorite snack, animal crackers. He quickly learned to select a photograph, put it in his book, and do the pictured activity, but he almost always chose matching, and rarely selected snack. When we introduced a second blank page and a second opportunity to choose, we added a photograph of a number-matching activity. Then he began to vary his choice of matching tasks, and often selected animal crackers when he encountered the second blank page.

Paula

Paula, now 10 years old, learned to follow a photographic schedule three years ago, and presently chooses from a large array of photographs displayed on a choice board. Her choices include playing several different computer games; watching segments of different videotapes; playing an electronic keyboard; using headphones to listen to music; preparing and eating snacks (for example, cheese and crackers, celery sticks filled with cream cheese, or bread and jelly); looking at books and magazines; playing card games (Uno and Slap Jack) with family members or peers; shooting baskets; and riding her bike. She sets a digital timer for specified amounts of time, and returns to her schedule when the timer rings. Frequent changes in the pictures displayed on her choice board appear to heighten her interest and promote conversation.

Teaching Children to Sequence Their Own Activities

After children have learned to select preferred activities, it is time to teach them to build their own schedules. We adults make ongoing decisions about what to do first and next. We may decide that, after attending to daily housekeeping chores and doing the laundry, we will do something more interesting, such as telephoning a relative or shopping for clothing. At work, we may review a boring report before beginning a more creative task. And sometimes, we avoid less-preferred jobs as long as possible: we weed a flower bed, get the mail, surf the Internet, and read a new magazine before doing the dishes and taking out the garbage. These decisions have an impact on the quality of day-to-day life.

Similarly, we can enhance the quality of life for young people with autism by teaching them to sequence their own activities. A child who selects reward activities from a choice board can also learn to select and sequence required activities.

To help her learn this skill, remove the photographs from the schedule book and attach them (with Velcro) to the inside front and back covers of a new three-ring binder of a different color. Then add one or more new pages to the schedule book to represent reward choices. If your daughter is a reader, the new pages may display the words "My choice"; if she does not yet read, display a photograph of the choice board.

Once again use graduated guidance, spatial fading, shadowing, and decreased proximity to help your daughter learn to open her new three-ring binder, select a photograph, mount the picture in her schedule book, obtain the materials, complete the activity, put materials away, return to her schedule book, turn the page, and open her new notebook to select a photograph of the next activity. When she is about to select a picture, use only the amount of manual guidance necessary to prevent errors. Minimal guidance will help her learn to choose.

At age four, Libby learned to sequence ten preschool activities. Photographs of preacademic, language, and leisure activities were mounted on the inside covers of a red binder. She selected a photograph from the red notebook, attached it to a page of her blue schedule book, obtained the necessary materials, completed the activity (sometimes with instruction from her teacher), put the materials away, and selected a different photograph. Pictures of her choice board in the blue schedule book cued her to select a picture from her choice board, attach it to the same page, and engage in a preferred activity. Her choice board included photographs of a slide, a hippety hop ball, Jello, balloons, and a top.

The number of opportunities to select rewards should reflect your child's current schedule-following skills. If your daughter recently completed a seven-page activity schedule in which the third and seventh pages presented opportunities to select a preferred activity, continue this schedule while you teach her to sequence her learning activities. And continue to deliver tokens that are exchanged for a special treat when the schedule is completed.

Teaching Children to Deliver Their Own Rewards

When your son consistently sequences his required activities and chooses among several preferred activities, teach him to deliver his own tokens. To accomplish this objective, attach the tokens or coins to the bottom of every page in his schedule and teach him to complete the activity, put materials away, remove the token or coin from the schedule page, place it on his token board, and then turn the page. When he has filled all of the Velcro dots on his clipboard, guide him to display the clipboard, and help him exchange his tokens for a special reward.

If your son attempts to "cheat" (takes tokens when he has not completed a scheduled activity or has incorrectly completed it), use the teaching procedures discussed earlier. Remove the token or coin that he did not earn, and guide him to continue his schedule.

As your youngster becomes more proficient, continue to add photographs to the three-ring binder and the choice board, and consider when to move tokens or coins from every page of his schedule book to every second page, and then every third page. Your data on schedule following will be helpful in making this decision.

Wes

Sixteen-year-old Wes, a member of a large family, follows a photographic schedule that begins when he arrives home from school at three o'clock, and ends at bedtime. His scheduled activities include dusting, vacuuming, making his school lunch for the next day, doing laundry, practicing typing skills, unloading the dishwasher, setting the table, interacting with family members, feeding the dog, doing homework, reporting on completed activities, and occasionally weeding, raking leaves, or shoveling snow.

Initially each of these tasks was presented in a separate photographic schedule. For example, making a school lunch was, at one time, a sixteen-page schedule that included pictures of a lunch bag, slices of bread, a knife, butter, lunch meat, cheese, a sandwich, a sandwich bag, vegetables, a plastic bag, fruit, a dessert, his initials on the lunch bag, putting the knife in the dishwasher, wiping the counter with a sponge, and putting the lunch bag in the refrigerator. When Wes learned this separate schedule, it was represented by a single picture in his main photographic schedule (a picture of a bulging lunch bag bearing his initials).

Over several years, Wes mastered many separate and lengthy schedules, and they are now represented by single photographs in his primary activity schedule, which is more than forty pages in length. He has acquired many leisure skills, and his recreational choices include in-line skating, biking, shooting baskets, kicking a soccer ball, jogging, preparing a variety of foods, swimming, watch-

ing TV, playing ping pong with family members, playing video games, completing puzzles, and using construction toys.

Wes selects and sequences all of his daily activities. It is noteworthy that he often chooses to complete all of his work assignments before engaging in leisure activities.

9 | From Pictures to Words

Lee

Because Lee could read a lot of sight words, we were able to use a number of toys that might not otherwise have been ideal candidates for his picture schedule. For example, we included a picture of a Playskool hammer bench with pegs of six different colors; we arranged the color words in different orders on the page, and taught him to hammer the pegs in the order listed in his schedule. We also used a photograph of Velcro play food that can be "cut" apart, with the words "cut the food," and different cards listing the foods to be cut. And we cut out a figure of a person, laminated it, and clothing of different colors, and displayed a picture of these materials with word cards that told him to "dress the boy," and listed the clothing to use (e.g., blue shirt, white socks). Lee likes singing, so we put cards in his schedule that say, "Mommy, sing the Alouette song" (and other songs he enjoys); this promotes interaction.

Introduction

Some children with autism quickly acquire reading skills, but most require a carefully programmed curriculum, such as the Edmark Reading Program (1992). Some youngsters develop early sight-word reading repertoires as a result of incidental teaching procedures (McGee, Krantz, & McClannahan, 1986), and others learn target words that are presented on flash cards during discrete-trial training sessions. Although many children learn to follow activity schedules before they begin to read, it is important to modify schedule books to recognize these new competencies as they develop. Learning to read enables your child to use a schedule that is more like your own.

Introducing Textual Cues

Sometimes after a child develops initial reading skills, words can be attached to the photographs in the schedule and, later, the pictures can be removed, with the result that the youngster responds to the words instead of the photographs. On the choice board shown in Figure 9-1, text was superimposed on the pictures. Later, the photographs were removed and only the words remained, and the youngster continued to do the scheduled activities.

But for other young people with autism, more systematic efforts are necessary to prepare them to use written schedules (McClannahan, 1998). Suppose that a youngster especially enjoys bite-size Mounds candy bars, and a picture of a Mounds bar is

(Fig. 9-1) On this choice board, words are superimposed on photographs.

(Fig. 9-2) Steps used to help a child make the transition from a photograph of a Mounds candy bar to the word "Mounds."

included in her schedule. The first step in the transition from photograph to text is to replace the color photo with a black-and-white photo or a photocopy of the candy wrapper. Some next steps are: (a) cut away small sections of the top and bottom of the candy wrapper, (b) cut away the sides of the wrapper, (c) cut away the small words "Peter Paul," and (d) cut away the line under the word (see Figure 9-2). Now only the word "Mounds" remains, but it is presented in a special type style. If you have a computer, you may experiment with different type sizes and fonts, to program a gradual transition to a typical type size and style. If you are not a computer user, you can achieve the same outcome by printing the word a little smaller on each presentation. Of course, each next step should be taken only if the child makes a correct response. If she is prompted, or obtains materials other than the Mounds bar, it is important to return to the previous step and provide practice opportunities.

The procedure described in the preceding paragraph is called stimulus fading. When designing stimulus-fading programs, it is important to identify stimuli that are and are not criterion related. Criterion-related stimuli are never faded; they are the stimuli that have an impact on your behavior, and they have an effect on the behavior of most people in our society. In our example, color and size are not criterion related because they will not help the child read the word "Mounds" when it appears on her choice board or on a flash card in a typical type size and type style. The word "Mounds" is criterion related. When they are well-designed, stimulus-fading programs result in fewer errors and faster learning (Etzel & LeBlanc, 1979).

Reading Skills and "To-Do" Lists

Reading skills create many new opportunities for independence and choice, because activities are more efficiently represented by words than by photographs. When a child begins to use textual rather than photographic cues, you may, at least for a while, continue the familiar format. Allow him to select activities from his choice board and notebook and place them in his schedule book. But when he is following his schedule with minimal errors, it is time to introduce the "to-do" list.

Using words that are mastered, sequence them in a list that will guide a series of responses. To-do lists may be used to cue household chores, food preparation, or self-care activities as well as homework, exercise, and social interaction tasks.

If a boy has paper-and-pencil skills, place a blank to the left of each item on the list, and teach him to check off each activity after it is accomplished (see Figure 9-3). If pencil use is a problem, put a Velcro dot to the left of each item, and teach him to move a coin or token to the next task in the list (see Figure 9-5). Teach to-do lists in the same way that you taught your child to use a photographic schedule. When you present the list for the first time, be prepared to use manual guidance, and use the familiar prompting and prompt-fading procedures.

Fig. 9-3 | To-Do List Example

To-do lists that cue household tasks, food preparation, and self-care. The youngster places a check mark to the left of each item after completing it.

Clean the Sink

_____ Get bucket from broom closet
_____ Put gloves on
_____ Take things off sink
_____ Spray mirror with Windex
_____ Wipe mirror with paper towel
_____ Look for streaks
_____ Spray sink with Windex
_____ Wipe with paper towel
_____ Look for dirt
_____ Put things back on sink
_____ Put Windex and towels in bucket
_____ Take off gloves
_____ Put gloves in bucket
_____ Put bucket in broom closet
_____ Wash hands
_____ Ask Mom, "How does the sink look?"

Pudding

_____ Wash hands
_____ Get bowl
_____ Get measuring cup
_____ Get milk
_____ Fill cup with milk
_____ Pour milk in dish
_____ Put measuring cup in dishwasher
_____ Put milk away
_____ Get box of pudding
_____ Get scissors
_____ Open box
_____ Cut bag open
_____ Put pudding mix in bowl
_____ Throw box away
_____ Put scissors away
_____ Get wisk
_____ Set timer for 2 minutes

(Continued on next page...)

(Figure 9-3 continued from previous page...)

_____ Stir pudding
_____ Turn timer off
_____ Put lid on bowl
_____ Put bowl in refrigerator
_____ Set timer for 5 minutes
_____ Put wisk in dishwasher
_____ Wipe counter
_____ Get 2 little bowls
_____ Get 2 napkins
_____ Get 2 little spoons
_____ Get one big spoon
_____ Ask Jimmy, "Do you want pudding?"

Shaving
_____ Get shaving kit
_____ Turn razor on
_____ Shave left cheek
_____ Shave right cheek
_____ Shave under nose
_____ Shave chin
_____ Shave neck
_____ Turn razor off
_____ Check for whiskers
_____ Clean razor
_____ Put razor in shaving kit
_____ Put shaving kit away
_____ Clean sink

Learning to use a to-do list is a key accomplishment! Many adults also use to-do lists to remind them of exercises during workouts, Saturday errands, grocery purchases, and phone calls.

Using Appointment Books

As reading and handwriting skills progress, some young people begin to use appointment books that are much like our own. Words that were previously presented on the choice board

(Fig. 9-4) When "Make salad" appears in his primary written activity schedule, Luke, age 12, obtains a special "to-do" list that serves as a recipe for making salad and dressing.

wash hands
get salad bowl
get lettuce
get knife
get cutting board
put lettuce back
get 1 tomato
put knife in sink
put cutting board in sink
get glass
get vinegar

or in a notebook are transferred to 3 x 5 note cards that are placed in a file box. Using the familiar instructional procedures, we manually guide the youth to remove the cards from the box, lay them on a work surface, sequence activities, and record them in an appointment book. After the schedule is constructed, we use manual guidance and prompt-fading to teach him to check off or cross out each activity after it is completed (see Figure 1-3, page 7).

Selection of an appointment book or daily planner may be determined by the size of a

Calisthenics

get weights
straddle stretch
pike stretch
butterfly stretch
10 sit ups
10 jumping jacks
10 arm presses
10 arm curls

(Fig. 9-5) A to-do list for a workout. After completing each task, the youth moves the coin to the next task.

young person's handwriting. If his writing is large, provide a desk-size planner and gradually diminish the space between lines. If his handwriting permits, buy a smaller appointment book. And after he learns to use this new schedule, teach him some other uses of appointment books, such as keeping track of holiday celebrations, family birthdays, school vacations, and other special events.

We know some youths who spend thirty minutes or more each day arranging note cards and constructing their own schedules. We do not view this as a problem, but as an indication that they care about their schedules.

10 | Expanding Social Interaction Skills

Introduction

Chapter 3 describes how to include social activities in children's first activity schedules. This chapter explains how to program more complex social interaction tasks. Of course, these endeavors will be most successful if you begin at your child's current language level.

Social Skills for Nonverbal Children

Youngsters who have not yet acquired speech can learn to initiate social activities. For example, you may teach a child to remove a picture of a swing, wagon, or bubbles from her schedule book, choice board, or notebook and give it to you as a means of beginning a social activity with you. Although she cannot yet talk, she can learn to seek you out, get your attention, and begin a social exchange, so that you can model conversation.

Later you may display photographs of family members or therapists on her choice board and teach her to select both the activity and the person with whom she will do it. Guide her to choose a photograph of an activity, select a photograph of a person, attach the picture of the person to the card on which the activity photo is mounted, and finally, seek out that family member and hand the card to him or her, as a means of beginning a social activity.

Offer social activities that your daughter enjoys. Depending on her preferences, you may read (or label pictures in) a favorite book, play with musical or noise-making toys, make block towers for her to knock over, play games with a flashlight, help her ride a trike, or jog her on your knees. If her visual attending skills are not yet well developed, you can build them by waiting for her to look at you before you accept the card and begin the activity she selected.

Social Skills for Children Who Say a Few Words

If you have other children, you know that typical preschoolers often say such things as, "Look," "Watch me," "What's that?" "Where's Daddy?" and "All done." These verbal productions can be included in youngsters' activity schedules, using a Language Master or audiotape recorder. This enables the child to initiate the interaction, and helps to diminish the likelihood that he will become dependent on verbal prompts from you.

Add one or two photographs of the Language Master to his activity schedule, and record models of the words you want him to imitate. Put the Language Master cards in the order that they will be used, and place them near the Language Master, in a basket or box.

If you record the word "Look," arrange his schedule book so that a photograph of the Language Master follows an activity that results in a product he can show you. For example, guide him to run the card through the Language Master, and then bring a completed coloring task, puzzle, or bristle block tower to you or another family member and say, "Look." If you record the words "Watch me," place the photo of the Language Master before a depicted activity for which you can be the audience, and teach him to imitate "Watch me" and then do a somersault, jump on a jogging trampoline, throw a ball, or run the truck down the ramp.

When he says "Look" or "Watch me," respond enthusiastically, but don't ask him for more language (this isn't a discrete-trial teaching session). Instead make statements that he can understand, and that you hope will be of interest to him (e.g., "You colored ice cream!" or "Barney puzzle!" or "Red fire truck!"). Then look expectantly at him, and wait to see if he has anything else to say (if he doesn't you can make another simple statement, such as "Barney is purple"). Research shows that over a period of time, he may combine your words with words he already knows, to produce new statements such as "Look, Barney" or "Big fire truck" (Krantz & McClannahan, 1998).

Use the familiar manual guidance and prompt-fading procedures to teach your child to use the Language Master, approach you, imitate the recorded words, and display a product or show you an activity. If he runs a card through the Language Master but doesn't imitate the recording, manually guide him to run the card through again (and again), but don't use verbal prompts. If you find that he is unable to imitate recorded words, consider providing discrete-trial training on imitating Language Master cards before putting them back in his schedule.

When your son masters the first social tasks, add more. A Language Master script such as "Where's Daddy?" may be an opportunity to take a walk around the house to find a parent who will provide a tickle or a toss in the air. And the script "Where's doggy?" may set the occasion to take a brief walk in the yard and play with the family pet.

Social Skills for Children Who Use Phrases and Sentences

Adults often speak about things they have done and things they are going to do; Language Master scripts or written scripts (if your child reads) can help youngsters do the same. For example, a child's activity schedule may cue her to report, "I'm going to cut," or "I finished handwriting." Data from the Princeton Child Development Institute's preschool and school suggest that, for children with sufficient language, providing several examples of a communication may help to expand language use. For ex-

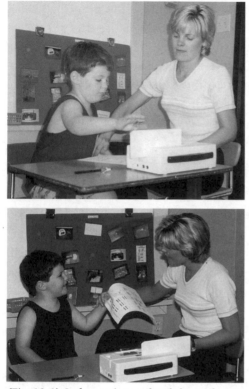

(Fig. 10-1) Jack, age 6, completed the arithmetic worksheet depicted in his schedule, selected and played a Language Master card, and imitated the script, "Math is fun!" Other audiotaped scripts he could have selected were "I'm good at math" and "I can add."

ample, the child who is about to use scissors and paste may select from one of three scripts: "I'm going to cut," "It's time to paste," and "I like to cut." And when cutting and pasting is completed, she may again select from three different communications, such as "Cutting is fun," "I finished cutting," and "Pasting is over."

Textual and auditory scripts help youngsters learn to give and receive information about themselves and others, and to enlist others' participation in activities. For example, a young child may imitate a Language Master card by saying "Let's go," or "Come with me" while taking the hand of a classmate or sibling and moving toward a depicted wagon or see-saw. Scripts such as "What are you doing?" or "What's this?" typically produce responses, not only from parents, but also from siblings, peers, and relatives. And children and youths with more speech or reading skills may initiate conversation with statements or questions such as "I like Burger King," "What's your favorite restaurant?" "Tony is my friend," "Do you have a pet?" or "Do you like music?"

Remember that these initiations should not be met with a barrage of questions, but with statements that the child is likely to understand and that are of interest to him. Children are more likely to learn that interaction is rewarding if we don't respond with difficult questions or demands for more language. Figure 10-2 shows a conversation between Ron, age 14, and his teacher. Ron enjoys camping with his family, and some of his previous Language Master scripts have addressed this topic. Note that the teacher does not ask questions or give directions, but guides the conversation in ways that encourage Ron's participation.

Fading Auditory and Textual Cues

After your child learns to use Language Master scripts or written words to initiate social interaction, help him take the next steps toward independence by gradually eliminating these cues. For ex-

---

Fig. 10-2 | Language Master Script

This conversation between Ron and his teacher was initiated by Ron, after he played a Language Master script. Note that the teacher does not ask questions or give directions, but makes statements that are of interest to Ron.

> **Ron:** (Says Language Master script). I go camping with Mom and Dad.
> **Teacher:** You have a sleeping bag.
> **Ron:** I sleep tent.
> **Teacher:** You camp by the river.
> **Ron:** By the river...I swim.
> **Teacher:** You're a good swimmer! (Then broadens topic to promote Ron's next response.) And you ride in the boat.
> **Ron:** Boat...I like boats.
> **Teacher:** I like boats, too. And I like to cook hot dogs when I camp.
> **Ron:** I like hot dogs.
> **Teacher:** I put mustard and catsup on my hot dogs.
> **Ron:** (No response after ten seconds)
> **Teacher:** It's nice talking to you.
> **Ron:** Nice talking to you. (Returns to schedule).

ample, if the Language Master recording was "What are you doing?" and he always says this script, begin by deleting the last word, so that the Language Master card now plays the words "What are you." If he continues to say the entire script on two or three occasions, delete another word, so that the card plays "What are." If he makes an error, return to the prior step ("What are you"), but if he correctly says the script on several opportunities, fade to "What." Eventually, erase "What" and provide a blank Language Master card. (Stevenson, Krantz, and McClannahan, 1998).

When encountering a blank card, many youngsters behave as though the Language Master is broken—they push the buttons and run the card through several times before they say the script. If your child does not abandon the blank card and say the script, use manual guidance to help him put the card away and turn toward you. If he still does not say the script, return to the previous step (a card that plays "What"). Finally, when your son says the script after running a blank card through the Language Master, add a new script and begin the process again, in order to teach him more conversation skills.

Script-fading procedures are similar for young readers. A girl who consistently reads the words "Do you like to sing?" next encounters the text "Do you like to," and if she continues to respond correctly, the script is faded to "Do you like" and so on, until only a generic cue (such as the word "Talk") remains in her activity schedule (Krantz & McClannahan, 1993).

Lee

At the end of his schedule, Lee finds the word "Talk." He comes over to one of us and talks about what he did: "Mommy, look what I did. I did the hammer, I did the food, I did the dressing, I did the pictures (a matching task), and I got to sing." He turns the pages in his schedule book while he talks, because he can't yet remember all of these things to tell us.

11 | Troubleshooting

Introduction

Many parents and teachers who help young people with autism learn to use activity schedules report some difficulties along the way. Teaching can be demanding, and it isn't always smooth sailing. This chapter discusses some frequently posed questions and concerns, and offers suggestions about how to deal with problems that are sometimes encountered during teaching.

He seems bored with the schedule.

Neither we nor young people with autism like to work on difficult tasks. But after we become proficient, we enjoy using and displaying our skills. If we want children to enjoy playing with toys, coloring, doing arithmetic worksheets, making snacks, or initiating interactions with others, we must provide multiple practice opportunities. If your son appears uninterested in activities that he has not yet mastered, continue to use the manual guidance and prompt-fading procedures until he meets the accuracy criteria. Later, after he develops relevant competencies, he may choose the activities that presently appear difficult or uninteresting.

Of course, when any learning problem is noted, it is always a good idea to review the available rewards, and to substitute new snacks, toys, games, or social activities for those that no longer appear interesting. If he is exchanging his tokens for Cheerios, try a different snack. If his schedule includes a toss in the air, consider replacing that activity with a "swing your partner" or "hang upside down" game. And as noted in Chapter 6, don't wait too long to change the order of activities in the schedule, or to introduce new activities.

She makes vocal noise or engages in motor stereotypy while doing her schedule.

One of the reasons for teaching schedule following is to help your child acquire new skills that are incompatible with vocal or motor stereotypy. If she hums, coos, repeats the same sound, or says a word or phrase over and over, remember that typical children are seldom silent during work and play activities. Continue to teach, but be especially careful not to deliver snacks, tokens, or other special rewards when she is displaying repetitive behavior.

If she attempts to engage in hand flapping, finger play, hand regarding, rocking, or other stereotyped motor behavior, return to manual guidance to prevent this behavior. The occurrence of repetitive motor responses is often predictable—one child may display stereotypic head turning each time she picks up laminated picture cards, another may flap his hands whenever a musical toy is activated, and a third may exhibit finger play before or after turning a page in the schedule book. If your observations permit you to predict the onset of stereotypy, you can use manual guidance to prevent it. If it reappears after you move to spatial fading, take this as an indication that fading began too soon and return to graduated guidance. Even if you can't predict and prevent dysfunctional motor responses, you can interrupt them quickly, so that there is little time to practice them.

He sometimes tantrums when we are teaching him to use his schedule.

It is unlikely that your son will learn much about his schedule while he is having a tantrum, and you probably don't want to risk having tantrum behavior become part of the new response sequences he is learning, so it's best to stop the schedule and do whatever you usually do about tantrums (for example, put him in a high chair, in his room, or on the bottom stair step until he is quiet and ready to follow directions).

If tantrums occur frequently, re-evaluate the rewards embedded in the schedule, and consider increasing the frequency of delivery of tokens, snacks, or especially enjoyable activities when he is performing well. But be careful not to teach him that having a tantrum prevents him from having to do his schedule; when the tantrum is over, begin the schedule again.

She takes pennies before she earns them.

Like us, children must learn that they may not take things that do not rightfully belong to them. Using token rewards is one way to teach your child this important principle, which will help her earn others' respect. Use manual guidance to prevent your youngster from taking coins, snacks, or other rewards not yet earned. But if she responds so quickly that you can't prevent her from grabbing a token, immediately remove it. If this behavior continues, you may decide not only to recover the token she grabbed, but to remove several additional coins or stickers and program an outcome in which she does not have the number of tokens needed to purchase the final snack or special activity.

Not uncommonly, children cooperate with token delivery during graduated guidance or spatial fading, but start to "steal" tokens when parents begin shadowing or decreasing physical proximity. This is a signal to return, at least temporarily, to the prior prompting procedure. When you once again begin to fade prompts, your daughter's behavior will tell you whether to continue the fading procedures.

My son has learned to use his schedule, but I have to stay in the room with him.

As noted in Chapter 6 (see New Problems, Familiar Solutions), fading adult proximity is perhaps the most difficult step in helping a child achieve real independence. Many children learn to follow several different schedules before they learn to pursue previously mastered activities in the absence of parents or teachers.

If after learning several schedules, your child is not successful when you are outside the room, there are several strategies you may explore. Try decreasing your proximity while engaging in another activity such as reading, folding laundry, or interacting with another family member. Although you continue to covertly observe his performance so that you can step in to prompt if needed, your scrutiny may be less relevant to him.

In addition if he is verbal, you may want to include additional social interaction tasks in his schedule, especially interactions that focus on task completion. Teach him to report to you after he completes each scheduled activity— for example, "I did puzzle" or "I made cheese crackers"—and praise and reward him for his independent work (or withhold praise and rewards if he completed the activity with prompts). Gradually move farther away when it is time for him to report so that, eventually, he must come to find you in another room.

Finally, move out of his sight for only a few seconds at a time, and time your return so that you can reward him for remaining engaged when you are absent. Then very gradually increase the number of seconds when you are not visible to him.

Of course, some scheduled activities are designed to be done in the presence of parents. Some youths' schedules include cues such as "Ask Dad to check my homework," or "Tell Mom it's time for language," or "Ask for help with arithmetic." Such scheduled activities create a platform for additional teaching—a parent may offer feedback on handwriting worksheets, provide discrete-trial training on articulation, or present flash cards that help a youth memorize addition facts.

If you use your son's schedule to remind you to review his homework assignments or help him with speech, you can maintain his growing independence by making him responsible for obtaining and putting away materials. Instead of telling him that it's time to put things away, simply indicate that the activity is over (e.g., "You're done with homework" or "We're finished with flash cards").

I can't always be home to do her schedule with her. Can I change it?

Some of us accept schedule changes better than others, but all of us must exhibit some flexibility. Changes in work schedules, changes in family members' commitments, and unexpected events often require us to juggle responsibilities and revise our plans. By teaching your daughter to use an activity schedule, you can teach her to tolerate changes in routine.

When necessary, don't hesitate to abbreviate your child's photographic or written schedule. If you must run errands or take another child to an after-school event, remove several pages from her schedule book and substitute a page that indicates a car ride. And after you have resequenced activities and she has mastered more than one schedule, feel free to add new components when this will help you respond to other obligations.

If you can anticipate certain schedule changes, prepare pictorial or textual cues in advance and provide practice opportunities when the daily routine is relatively forgiving. For example, add photographs that indicate meeting a parent at the train or bus station; taking a sibling to soccer practice; going to the mall, to the pediatrician, or to grandma's house; watching TV; bathing; or going to bed. Delete usual activities and add these alternate activities from time to time, even when circumstances do not require that you do so. This will not only contribute to the quality of life for other family members, but will also help your youngster with autism learn to accept change and make positive contributions to your family. An activity schedule is merely a tool. Make ongoing decisions about your daughter's daily schedule, just as you make decisions about other aspects of her education and family participation.

We're so busy that I can hardly find time to set up his schedule each day.

As a parent of a child with autism, you have learned many coping skills that help you deal with the demands of everyday life. Teaching your son to use an activity schedule initially increases those demands, but ultimately creates some freedom for you. Some advance attention to the design of his work and play environment will help you reap these rewards. Chapter 3 discusses arrangements of materials that contribute to young people's independence.

Given a well-designed learning environment, you can not only teach your boy to use an activity schedule, but also to assume responsibility for his possessions. If there is a designated place for work and play materials, the teaching procedures will enable him to put things away. When you begin a new schedule, don't hesitate to manually guide him to do a few "extra" activities that are not shown in the photographs or elaborated in the text. If he builds a K'Nex model, guide him to disassemble it and put the pieces back in the bin before he puts it away. If he cuts with scissors, guide him to pick up scraps of paper and throw them in the wastebasket. If he makes pudding, teach him to finish by wiping the counter and putting utensils in the dishwasher.

Ultimately activity schedules achieve useful outcomes only if we use the teaching procedures to enable children to exhibit criterion performances; that is, to complete target activities skillfully and correctly, so that others don't have to accept inadequate performances or re-do tasks later. Learning to make meatloaf is a functional skill only if the activity does not create more work for others, and only if the meatloaf tastes good and contributes to the family dinner. Learning to vacuum the carpet is useful only if the carpet is clean at the end of the activity. And learning to use an activity schedule is most useful when young people learn to manage their own schedules and materials. All of these important outcomes are accomplished by using the teaching procedures described earlier.

I'm worried that the activity schedule is adding to my child's social isolation.

Some young schedule users appear very engrossed in planned activities, and may even ignore others who are nearby. Many children, like us, prefer not to be interrupted during nonsocial tasks such as using the computer, reading or looking at books or magazines, completing worksheets, or cooking. But if your child attempts to isolate herself during social activities—for example, avoids looking at you while talking to you, or while receiving a tickle—you may want to add more social activities to her schedule and provide rewards only when she interacts and looks at others. As noted earlier, social interaction is a key deficit for children with autism; multiple practice opportunities, followed by powerful rewards, help build social competence.

My child seems to want manual guidance all of the time. How can I fade prompts?

Many youngsters appear to enjoy physical contact, perhaps because of parents' efforts to draw them into a social world. And some children wait to be manually guided because they have learned to depend upon adults' prompts (see Chapter 4—Why Manual Guidance?). If your child waits to be prompted, magnify your physical contact with him. Consider adding tickling, wrestling, hugging, and roughhousing, both as scheduled activities, and as rewards that are earned at the end of the schedule. Deliver a minimum of these activities when he waits to be prompted, and offer intensive, lengthy physical contact when he is performing well.

Our preschooler has trouble turning the pages of her schedule.

It's not unusual for a child to develop schedule-following skills before acquiring the manual dexterity needed to turn pages, and it's quite acceptable to devise temporary alternatives. Some youngsters learn to use large tabs attached to the right side of each page, enabling them to turn one page at a time. Others succeed at page turning if we attach Velcro to the bottom of each page (this separates pages, making it easier to grasp a single page).

My son still doesn't have picture-object correspondence skills. What should I do?

Learning picture-object correspondence is sometimes a major hurdle. We have known children who mastered this skill only after several years of instruction. In the meantime, we bypassed the issue and helped them become schedule users by focusing on their matching skills. If a youngster can match pictures, put one picture in his schedule book and attach an identical picture to a bin that contains the relevant materials. If he can match alphabet letters or numerals, put letters or numerals in his schedule book and attach corresponding letters or numerals to baskets that contain toys or learning activities. If he hasn't yet learned to match two-dimensional stimuli but can match objects, mount objects in his book and on containers. For example, put a real puzzle piece in his book, and attach an identical puzzle piece to the puzzle container. We know youngsters who learned to take bathroom breaks or ride tricycles when doll-furniture toilets and trikes were attached to schedule pages. Continue to work on picture-object correspondence—these skills make important contributions to independence.

How long should we wait before we prompt?

We often feel impaled on the horns of this dilemma. If we prompt too soon, we prevent a young person from enjoying independent task completion. If we prompt too late, she may make an error that will appear again and again. When to prompt is a judgment that each of us must make on the basis of previous observation. If she usually completes this task independently, it is likely that she will do that again, even after a pause of ten or fifteen seconds. If this is a difficult task (one that usually requires assistance), prompt quickly, before she forgets what she is doing or engages in an inappropriate behavior. Observation of her current performance offers the best guidelines about when to prompt.

He pushes cards through the Language Master, making them sound garbled.

Experimentation is typical of children with and without developmental disabilities. A majority of young schedule users experiment with the Language Master—they push various buttons, attempt to unplug it, and manipulate cards as they are playing. Our responsibilities include teaching children appropriate use of the Language Master, just as we teach them how to use the television, bathtub, and screen door. If your youngster incorrectly uses the Language Master, return to manual guidance; when he is correctly using this learning tool, again fade your prompts. And don't forget to record new cards when the originals wear out, play faintly, or present unclear models.

Ken

We have known Ken since he was three, and autism is only one of his diagnoses. He is severely developmentally disabled, takes seizure-control medications that often produce undesirable side effects, and has long-standing health problems. Now twenty-five years old, he did not learn to follow a photographic activity schedule until he was sixteen, when this technology became available, but it made an important difference in his life. His schedule cues him to do personal hygiene tasks, to help with household chores such as setting the table and cleaning his room, and to choose leisure activities. At work, his schedule helps him count and package parts used in the automotive industry, and enables him to select among a variety of options about how to spend break time. Social interactions are included in his schedules and although his vocabulary is limited, he enthusiastically approaches others for discussions of his plans for days off, for visiting relatives, or going to favorite restaurants. He is pleasant and productive, and we look forward to our conversations with him. Although we can't measure happiness, he appears to us to be happy.

APPENDIX A
Prerequisite Skills Data Sheet

Prerequisite Skills Data Sheet for _____

Opportunity#	Task	Date/Time	Date/Time	Date/Time
	Picture Versus Background			
1				
2				
3				
4				
5				
6				
7				
8				
9				
10				
Number Correct				

(Continued on next page)

Opportunity#	Task	Date/Time	Date/Time	Date/Time
	Matching Identical Objects			
1				
2				
3				
4				
5				
6				
7				
8				
9				
10				
Number Correct				

Opportunity#	Task	Date/Time	Date/Time	Date/Time
	Picture-Object Correspondence			
1				
2				
3				
4				
5				
Number Correct				

APPENDIX B
Data Sheet

OBSERVER:					
DATE:					
Activity	Opens Book/ Turns Page	Points/ Looks	Obtains	Completes	Puts Away
# Completed					
Number of components correctly completed:					
Total number of components:					
Percentage of components correctly completed:					

OBSERVER:					
DATE:					
Activity	Opens Book/ Turns Page	Points/ Looks	Obtains	Completes	Puts Away
# Completed					
Number of components correctly completed:					
Total number of components:					
Percentage of components correctly completed:					

APPENDIX C
Language Master

Language Master machines and Language Master cards may be ordered from EIKI International, Inc., 26794 Vista Terrace Drive, Lake Forest, CA 92630 (714-457-0200). The Portable Card Reader (VCR-LM1) costs approximately $225.00. A/C adapter and blank cards are available separately.

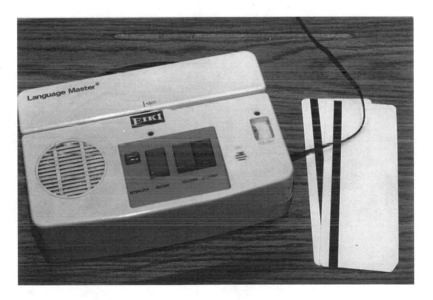

INDEX

ABOUT THE AUTHORS

Drs. Lynn E. McClannahan and Patricia J. Krantz are Executive Directors of the Princeton Child Development Institute, a community-based, nonprofit program that offers science-based services to children, youths, and adults with autism. They are the authors of many journal articles and book chapters, and their applied behavior analysis research on autism intervention is recognized both nationally and internationally.

Lovaas, O. I. *The Autistic Child: Language Development through Behavior Modification.* New York: Irvington, 1977.

Lutzker, J. R., McGimsey-McRae, S., & McGimsey, J. F. "General Description of Behavioral Approaches." In *Behavior Therapy for the Developmentally and Physically Disabled.* Edited by M. Hersen, V. B. VanHasselt, & J. L. Matson. (p. 42). New York: Academic Press, 1983.

MacDuff, G. S., Krantz, P. J., & McClannahan, L. E. "Teaching Children with Autism to Use Photographic Activity Schedules: Maintenance and Generalization of Complex Response Chains." *Journal of Applied Behavior Analysis 26* (1993): 89-97.

McClannahan, L. E. "From Photographic to Textual Cues." In *Teaching Independence and Choice: Design, Implementation, and Assessment of the Use of Activity Schedules.* By P. J. Krantz, G. S. MacDuff, E. C. Fenske, & L. E. McClannahan. Princeton, NJ: Princeton Child Development Institute, 1998. Videotapes.

McClannahan, L. E. & Krantz, P. J. "In Search of Solutions to Prompt Dependence: Teaching Children with Autism to Use Photographic Activity Schedules." In *Environment and Behavior.* Edited by E. M. Pinkston & D. M. Baer. Boulder, CO: Westview Press, 1997.

McGee, G. G., Krantz, P. J., & McClannahan, L. E. "An Extension of Incidental Teaching Procedures to Reading Instruction for Autistic Children." *Journal of Applied Behavior Analysis 19* (1986): 147-57.

Stevenson, C. L., Krantz, P. J., & McClannahan, L. E. *Teaching Children with Autism to Interact: Fading Audiotaped Scripts.* (Unpublished manuscript, 1998).

REFERENCES

Cooper, J. O. "Stimulus Control." In *Applied Behavior Analysis.* Edited by J. O. Cooper, T. E. Heron, & W. L. Heward. (p. 315). Columbus, OH: Merrill Publishing Co., 1987.

Edmark Corporation. *Edmark Reading Program,* 2nd ed. Redmond, WA: Edmark Corp., 1992.

Etzel, B. C. & LeBlanc, J. M. "The Simplest Treatment Alternative: The Law of Parsimony Applied to Choosing Appropriate Instructional Control and Errorless-Learning Procedures for the Difficult-to-Teach Child." *Journal of Autism and Developmental Disorders 9* (1979): 361-82.

Krantz, P. J., MacDuff, M. T., & McClannahan, L. E. "Programming Participation in Family Activities for Children with Autism: Parents' Use of Photographic Activity Schedules." *Journal of Applied Behavior Analysis 26* (1993): 137-38.

Krantz, P. J. & McClannahan, L. E. "Teaching Children with Autism to Initiate to Peers: Effects of a Script-Fading Procedure." *Journal of Applied Behavior Analysis 26* (1993): 121-32.

Krantz, P. J. & McClannahan, L. E. "Social Interaction Skills for Children with Autism: A Script-Fading Procedure for Beginning Readers." *Journal of Applied Behavior Analysis 31* (1998): 191-202.